KB087215

초등 영어 교재의 베스트셀러

초등 영어 문법 실력 쌓기!

Grammar Builder

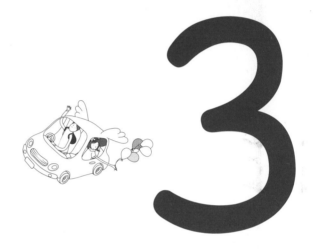

3

Grammar Builder 3

ⓒ2015 by I am Books

지은이	이상건
펴낸이	신성현, 오상욱
관리	허윤정
펴낸곳	도서출판 아이엠북스
	153-802 서울시 금천구 가산디지털2로 14 1116호 (대륭테크노타운 12차)
대표전화	02-6343-0999
팩스	02-6343-0995
출판등록	2006년 6월 7일
	제 313-2006-000122호
ISBN	978-89-6398-099-7 63740

저자와의 협의에 따라 인지는 붙이지 않습니다. 잘못된 책은 구입하신 곳에서 교환해 드립니다.
이 책에 게재된 내용의 일부 또는 전체를 무단으로 복제 및 발췌하는 것을 금합니다.

www.iambooks.co.kr

초등 영어 교재의 베스트셀러

초등 영어 문법 실력 쌓기!

Grammar Builder

You Are the Only One!

3

Introduction

Grammar Builder는?

이 책의 성격

문법 개념 설명부터 마무리 확인까지 실용 문제로 구성된 기본 영어 문법서

이 책의 학습 목표 및 특징

- 다양하고 많은 문제를 통해 실전 문법을 익히고 영어 교과 과정을 대비한다.
- 이해하기 쉽게 설명한 문법의 개념과 원리를 바탕으로 문제를 통해 실력을 향상시킨다.
- 핵심 문법 개념을 이해하고 점진적으로 확장된 문제를 통해 문법 원리를 익힌다.
- 문법 학습뿐만 아니라 문장 패턴 학습과 기초 문장 영작을 통해 문장 쓰기를 훈련한다.
- 서술형 비중이 커지는 추세를 반영하여 학업 성취도 및 서술형 평가를 대비한다.

이 책에 대한 세부 사항

- 문법 개념 설명부터 마무리 확인까지 문제 형식으로 구성하여 실전에 강하도록 하였다.
- 선택형 문제, 단답형 쓰기, 문장 패턴 쓰기로 확장하며 실력을 향상하도록 구성하였다.
- 단어와 문장을 정리하여 사전에 학습함으로 자연스럽게 문법 학습이 이루어지도록 하였다.
- 실전 문제와 서술형 문제를 강화하여 문법 개념과 원리를 응용할 수 있도록 하였다.

이 책을 활용한 영어 문법 실력 쌓기

1. 문법 학습 전 정리된 단어와 문장을 먼저 예습한다.
   - 단어와 문장을 알면 어렵게 느껴지는 문법도 쉽게 학습할 수 있다.

2. 문법은 이해＋암기이다. 필요한 문법 사항은 암기한다.
   - 문법의 쓰임과 역할을 이해하고 암기하여 필요할 때 적용하는 것이 좋다.

3. 문법을 학습할 때 예문을 통해 문법 개념을 학습한다.
   - 예문을 문법적으로 파악하면 문장이 복잡해도 쉽게 이해할 수 있다.

4. 문제를 푸는 것으로 끝내지 않고 대화나 글로 마무리한다.
   - 문법을 배우는 이유는 글을 이해하고 쓸 수 있는 능력을 갖추기 위한 것이다.

Grammar Series Contents

 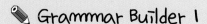

contents

About This Book  구성 및 특징

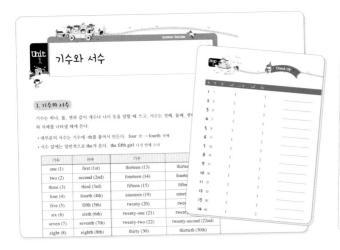

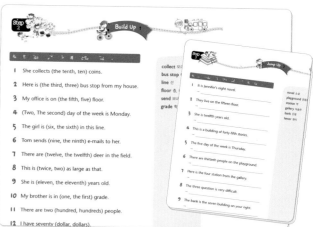

1. Unit별 핵심 문법 개념 정리

Unit별 학습목표를 제시하여 중점 사항을 파악하도록 하였고, 기초적인 문법 사항을 쉽게 이해할 수 있도록 설명하여 문법 개념 이해를 돕습니다. 또한 다양한 예문을 통해 문법 원리 학습을 적용하여 이해하도록 하였습니다.

2. Step 1 – Check Up

학습목표와 핵심문법 개념에 대한 기초적인 확인 문제로 구성하여 문법 원리를 문제를 통해서 익히도록 구성하였습니다. 스스로 풀어보면서 반복 학습을 통해 문법의 규칙을 이해하도록 하였습니다.

3. Step 2 – Build Up

다양한 형식의 다소 난이도 있는 문제로 구성하여 앞에서 배운 내용을 복습하며 문법 원리를 익히도록 하였습니다. 학습한 내용을 본격적으로 적용하고 응용해 보면서 다양한 유형을 연습하도록 하였습니다.

4. Step 3 – Jump Up

핵심 문법 개념을 스스로 정리해 보도록 하여 이해도를 확인하고 보완하도록 하였으며 확장형 응용문제를 통해 학습 목표를 성취하도록 하였습니다. 또한 영작문 실력이 향상되도록 서술형 문제 위주로 구성하였습니다.

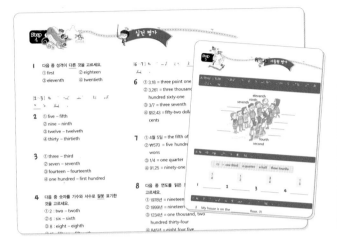

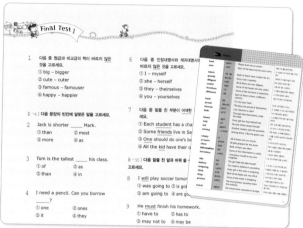

5. Step 4 – 실전 평가

Unit별 핵심 문법 개념과 다양한 문제로 익힌 문법 사항을 마무리 테스트로 구성하여 스스로 점검해 보도록 하였습니다. 이를 통해 문법 문제에 대한 응용력을 키우고 시험 유형에 대비하도록 하였습니다.

6. Step 5 – 서술형 평가

점점 서술형 비중이 커지는 추세를 반영하여 영작문 위주로 구성된 Unit별 종합 문제를 풀어보면서 Unit을 정리하고 학업성취도 평가 및 서술형 평가를 대비하도록 하였습니다.

7. Final Test

본 교재를 통해서 배운 핵심 문법 개념과 문법 사항을 종합평가로 풀어보면서 정리하고 마무리하도록 하였습니다. 종합적으로 배운 내용을 확인하고 점검하도록 하였습니다.

8. Words in Grammar

본 교재의 본문에 사용된 단어들과 문장을 정리하여 문법 학습에 활용하도록 하였습니다. 예습으로 단어를 학습하고 학습 집중도를 올리도록 활용하는 것이 좋습니다.

Curriculum 이 책의 활용법

Book	Month	Week	Hour	Unit	
1	1	1	1	1. 문장의 기본 구성	Words 활용
			2		서술형 평가
		2	1	2. 셀 수 있는 명사	Words 활용
			2		서술형 평가
		3	1	3. 셀 수 없는 명사	Words 활용
			2		서술형 평가
		4	1	4. 관사	Words 활용
			2		서술형 평가
	2	1	1	5. 인칭대명사와 격변화	Words 활용
			2		서술형 평가
		2	1	6. 지시대명사, 지시형용사	Words 활용
			2		서술형 평가
		3	1	7. be동사의 현재시제	Words 활용
			2		서술형 평가
		4	1	8. be동사의 부정문, 의문문	Words 활용
			2		서술형 평가
2	3	1	1	1. 일반동사의 현재시제	Words 활용
			2		서술형 평가
		2	1	2. 일반동사의 부정문, 의문문	Words 활용
			2		서술형 평가
		3	1	3. There is/are, 비인칭주어 it	Words 활용
			2		서술형 평가
		4	1	4. 형용사	Words 활용
			2		서술형 평가
	4	1	1	5. Some, Any, All, Every	Words 활용
			2		서술형 평가
		2	1	6. 수량형용사	Words 활용
			2		서술형 평가
		3	1	7. 부사	Words 활용
			2		서술형 평가
		4	1	8. 현재진행형	Words 활용
			2		서술형 평가
3	5	1	1	1. 기수와 서수	Words 활용
			2		서술형 평가
		2	1	2. 부정대명사, 재귀대명사	Words 활용
			2		서술형 평가
		3	1	3. 비교 구문	Words 활용
			2		서술형 평가
		4	1	4. 조동사	Words 활용
			2		서술형 평가

Grammar Builder 시리즈는 총 5권으로 구성되어 있으며, 권당 8주(2개월) 16차시(Unit당 2차시 수업)로 학습할 수 있도록 구성하였습니다. 주 2회 수업을 기준으로 하였으며 학습자와 학습 시간에 따라 변경이 가능합니다.

Book	Month	Week	Hour	Unit	
3	6	1	1	5. 동사의 과거시제	Words 활용
			2		서술형 평가
		2	1	6. 과거시제의 부정문, 의문문	Words 활용
			2		서술형 평가
		3	1	7. 과거진행형	Words 활용
			2		서술형 평가
		4	1	8. 동사의 미래시제	Words 활용
			2		서술형 평가
4	7	1	1	1. 의문사 의문문	Words 활용
			2		서술형 평가
		2	1	2. 의문대명사와 의문형용사	Words 활용
			2		서술형 평가
		3	1	3. 의문부사	Words 활용
			2		서술형 평가
		4	1	4. 명령문	Words 활용
			2		서술형 평가
	8	1	1	5. 감탄문	Words 활용
			2		서술형 평가
		2	1	6. 접속사	Words 활용
			2		서술형 평가
		3	1	7. 전치사	Words 활용
			2		서술형 평가
		4	1	8. 부정의문문, 부가의문문	Words 활용
			2		서술형 평가
5	9	1	1	1. to부정사	Words 활용
			2		서술형 평가
		2	1	2. 동명사	Words 활용
			2		서술형 평가
		3	1	3. 현재분사와 과거분사	Words 활용
			2		서술형 평가
		4	1	4. 문장의 형식 1	Words 활용
			2		서술형 평가
	10	1	1	5. 문장의 형식 2	Words 활용
			2		서술형 평가
		2	1	6. 현재완료	Words 활용
			2		서술형 평가
		3	1	7. 수동태	Words 활용
			2		서술형 평가
		4	1	8. 관계대명사	Words 활용
			2		서술형 평가

기수와 서수

개수를 나타내는 말과 순서를 나타내는 말을 이해할 수 있다.

영어로 숫자를 읽고 쓰는 방법을 알고 잘 활용할 수 있다.

기수는 하나, 둘, 셋과 같이 개수나 나이 등을 말할 때 쓰고, 서수는 첫째, 둘째, 셋째와 같이 순서나 차례를 나타낼 때 써요. 대부분의 서수는 기수에 -th를 붙여서 만들며 서수 앞에 일반적으로 the가 와요.

Unit
1

기수와 서수

1. 기수와 서수

기수는 하나, 둘, 셋과 같이 개수나 나이 등을 말할 때 쓰고, 서수는 첫째, 둘째, 셋째와 같이 순서와 차례를 나타낼 때에 쓴다.

- 대부분의 서수는 기수에 -th를 붙여서 만든다. **four** 넷 → **fourth** 넷째
- 서수 앞에는 일반적으로 the가 온다. **the fifth girl** 다섯 번째 소녀

기수	서수	기수	서수
one (1)	first (1st)	thirteen (13)	thirteenth (13th)
two (2)	second (2nd)	fourteen (14)	fourteenth (14th)
three (3)	third (3rd)	fifteen (15)	fifteenth (15th)
four (4)	fourth (4th)	nineteen (19)	nineteenth (19th)
five (5)	fifth (5th)	twenty (20)	twentieth (20th)
six (6)	sixth (6th)	twenty-one (21)	twenty-first (21st)
seven (7)	seventh (7th)	twenty-two (22)	twenty-second (22nd)
eight (8)	eighth (8th)	thirty (30)	thirtieth (30th)
nine (9)	ninth (9th)	forty (40)	fortieth (40th)
ten (10)	tenth (10th)	ninety (90)	ninetieth (90th)
eleven (11)	eleventh (11th)	one hundred (100)	one hundredth (100th)
twelve (12)	twelfth (12th)	one thousand (1,000)	one thousandth (1,000th)

four
fourth

lesson one → 1과, **the first lesson** 첫 번째 과

There are five boys **on the playground.** 운동장에 5명의 소년들이 있다.

The girl is the fifth student **in this line.** 그 소녀는 이 줄에서 5번째 학생이다.

2. 배수

배수는 '(~보다) ~배'를 나타낼 때 사용하며 3배부터는 기수에 **times**를 붙여서 사용한다.

twice 2배, **three times** 3배, **four times** 4배

This is twice as large as that. 이것은 저것보다 2배 더 크다.

Pop Quiz   I. 다음 기수를 서수로 고쳐 쓰세요.

❶ two → _____   ❷ twelve → _____   ❸ twenty → _____

3. 여러 가지 수 읽기

(1) 연도: 연도는 일반적으로 두 자리씩 끊어서 읽는다.

1997 → nineteen(19) ninety-seven(97)

2007 → two thousand (and) seven

(2) 날짜: 우리말은 년/월/일/요일로 나타내지만 영어에서는 요일/월/일/년의 순서로 나타낸다. of를 사용할 경우에는 the + 서수로 써야 한다.

4월 5일 → April (the) five(fifth), the fifth of April

1981년 4월 5일 → April (the) five(fifth), nineteen eighty-one

1981년 4월 5일 일요일 → Sunday (the) April five(fifth), nineteen eighty-one

(3) 전화번호: 하나씩 기수로 읽는다. 0은 o[ou]라고 읽는 것이 보통이지만 zero라고도 읽는다.

208-7463 → two o[ou] eight seven four six three

(02) 123-4567 → area code zero two, one two three four five six seven

(4) 돈, 화폐: 숫자와 함께 화폐 단위를 붙여서 읽는다.

$7.25 → seven dollars (and) twenty-five cents

₩520 → five hundred and twenty won

지역 번호는 area code를 붙여 읽고, 맨 앞자리가 숫자 0인 경우 zero라고 읽는다.

(5) 소수점: 소수점까지는 기수로 읽고 소수점은 point로 읽는다. 소수점 이하는 기수로 하나씩 읽는다.

21.27 → twenty-one point two seven

(6) 분수: 분자는 기수로 읽고, 분모는 서수로 읽는다.

분자가 2 이상이면 분모는 복수형으로 읽는다.

$\frac{1}{2}$ → a half, one half $\frac{1}{3}$ → a third, one third

$\frac{2}{3}$ → two thirds $\frac{1}{4}$ → a quarter, one fourth

$2\frac{2}{3}$
→ two and two thirds

Pop Quiz   2. 다음 숫자를 영어로 쓰세요.

❶ 8.35 → _____   ❷ $\frac{2}{3}$ → _____

다음 괄호 안에는 기수를, 밑줄에는 서수를 쓰세요.

1 1   (   )   _____

2 3   (   )   _____

3 5   (   )   _____

4 7   (   )   _____

5 9   (   )   _____

6 11   (   )   _____

7 13   (   )   _____

8 15   (   )   _____

9 17   (   )   _____

10 19   (   )   _____

11 21   (   )   _____

12 23   (   )   _____

13 30   (   )   _____

14 50   (   )   _____

15 70   (   )   _____

16 100   (   )   _____

다음 괄호 안에는 기수를, 밑줄에는 서수를 쓰세요.

1 2   (   )   _____

2 4   (   )   _____

3 6   (   )   _____

4 8   (   )   _____

5 10   (   )   _____

6 12   (   )   _____

7 14   (   )   _____

8 16   (   )   _____

9 18   (   )   _____

10 20   (   )   _____

11 22   (   )   _____

12 24   (   )   _____

13 40   (   )   _____

14 60   (   )   _____

15 80   (   )   _____

16 1,000 (   )   _____

다음 연도나 날짜를 영어로 쓰세요.

1 1984년 → _____

2 6월 15일 → _____

3 1991년 → _____

4 2000년 5월 4일 → _____

5 10월 7일 → _____

6 1970년 → _____

7 2000년 12월 25일 → _____

8 1352년 → _____

9 9월 10일 → _____

10 1845년 → _____

11 2008년 → _____

12 4월 2일 → _____

13 2012년 7월 7일 → _____

14 5월 5일 → _____

15 1253년 → _____

16 1974년 → _____

January 1월
February 2월
March 3월
April 4월
May 5월
June 6월
July 7월
August 8월
September 9월
October 10월
November 11월
December 12월

다음 전화번호와 금액을 영어로 쓰세요.

I ☎ 538–4725 → _____

2 ☎ 304–1286 → _____

3 $32.25 → _____

4 ₩750 → _____

5 ☎ (02) 492–5247 → _____

6 ☎ (053) 258–1284 → _____

7 $58.15 → _____

8 $18.57 → _____

9 ₩5,490 → _____

IO ☎ 284–3614 → _____

II ☎ 851–2040 → _____

I2 $99.40 → _____

I3 ₩9,990 → _____

I4 ☎ (031) 241–8506 → _____

I5 $450.10 → _____

I6 ☎ 334–1852 → _____

다음 분수나 소수점 또는 배수를 영어로 쓰세요.

point 점, 소수점
time 몇 번, 배
half 반, 2분의 1
quarter 4분의 1

1 $\frac{2}{5}$ → _____

2 $\frac{1}{3}$ → _____

3 75.26 → _____

4 12.854 → _____

5 5배 → _____

6 2배 → _____

7 5.07 → _____

8 $\frac{1}{4}$ → _____

9 $2\frac{2}{3}$ → _____

10 10배 → _____

11 $3\frac{3}{4}$ → _____

12 $\frac{1}{2}$ → _____

13 0.24 → _____

14 9.99 → _____

15 12배 → _____

16 $4\frac{1}{5}$ → _____

다음 여러 가지 숫자 표기를 영어로 쓰세요.

1 ☎ 382-9201 → _____

2 1845년 → _____

3 24번째 → _____

4 44.85 → _____

5 $\frac{3}{7}$ → _____

6 $65.20 → _____

7 $8.75 → _____

8 8월 15일 → _____

9 ₩950 → _____

10 3배 → _____

11 30번째 → _____

12 $9.10 → _____

13 ₩2,500 → _____

14 1950년 → _____

15 9월 23일 → _____

16 ☎ 985-4176 → _____

다음 괄호 안에서 알맞은 것을 골라 동그라미 하세요.

1 She collects (the tenth, ten) coins.

2 Here is (the third, three) bus stop from my house.

3 My office is on (the fifth, five) floor.

4 (Two, The second) day of the week is Monday.

5 The girl is (six, the sixth) in this line.

6 Tom sends (nine, the ninth) e-mails to her.

7 There are (twelve, the twelfth) deer in the field.

8 This is (twice, two) as large as that.

9 She is (eleven, the eleventh) years old.

10 My brother is in (one, the first) grade.

11 There are two (hundred, hundreds) people.

12 I have seventy (dollar, dollars).

13 Two (third, thirds) of the students are boys.

14 My birthday is on (five, the fifth) of October.

15 The hospital is on (three, the third) floor.

16 The man and woman have (two, second) sons.

collect 모으다
bus stop 버스 정류장
line 선
floor 층, 마루
send 보내다
grade 학년, 등급

다음 괄호 안의 숫자를 기수 또는 서수로 알맞게 쓰세요.

basket 바구니
postcard 엽서
meal 식사
finger 손가락
minute 분
Arbor Day 식목일
story 층

1 There is _____ apple in the basket. (1)

2 The _____ day of the week is Tuesday. (3)

3 Max sends _____ postcards to the friends. (9)

4 I have _____ sisters and brothers. (4)

5 We have _____ fingers. (10)

6 This is her _____ meal today. (3)

7 It takes _____ minutes to get there by car. (30)

8 Olivia is the _____ student in the line. (2)

9 The _____ question is very easy. (7)

10 I ask you _____ questions from Part B. (5)

11 We pay _____ dollars for the pants. (18)

12 It is Peter's _____ comic book. (6)

13 We plant _____ trees on Arbor Day. (50)

14 Jenny and Eric meet at _____ o'clock. (3)

15 This is a building of _____ stories. (63)

16 Christmas is on the _____ of December. (25)

다음 괄호 안의 숫자를 기수 또는 서수로 알맞게 쓰세요.

1 Please push the _____ button. (2)

2 Go straight _____ blocks and you can find it. (4)

3 They live on the _____ floor. (7)

4 My mother is _____ years old. (42)

5 This is her _____ album. (12)

6 There are _____ bedrooms in our house. (2)

7 It is the _____ building on your right. (5)

8 September is the _____ month of this year. (9)

9 We live in Seoul for _____ years. (11)

10 This music is her _____ Symphony. (6)

11 Today is our _____ wedding anniversary. (30)

12 She gives _____ dollars to me. (100)

13 Amy and Mark have _____ dogs. (8)

14 You and I are in the _____ grade. (3)

15 It is _____ kilometers from here to Jeju. (13)

16 Thanksgiving Day is the _____ Thursday of November. (4)

button 단추, 버튼
block 블록, 구역
left 왼쪽
symphony 심포니
anniversary 기념일

다음 빈칸에 알맞은 말을 쓰세요.

1 기수와 서수

기수	서수	기수	서수
one (1)	_____ (1st)	thirteen (13)	_____ (13th)
two (2)	_____ (2nd)	fourteen (14)	_____ (14th)
three (3)	_____ (3rd)	fifteen (15)	_____ (15th)
four (4)	_____ (4th)	nineteen (19)	_____ (19th)
five (5)	_____ (5th)	twenty (20)	_____ (20th)
six (6)	_____ (6th)	twenty-one (21)	_____ (21st)
seven (7)	_____ (7th)	twenty-two (22)	_____ (22nd)
eight (8)	_____ (8th)	thirty (30)	_____ (30th)
nine (9)	_____ (9th)	forty (40)	_____ (40th)
ten (10)	_____ (10th)	ninety (90)	_____ (90th)
eleven (11)	_____ (11th)	one hundred (100)	_____ (100th)
twelve (12)	_____ (12th)	one thousand (1,000)	_____ (1,000th)

2 여러 가지 수 읽기

(1) **연도:** 연도는 일반적으로 두 자리씩 끊어서 읽는다.

(2) **날짜:** 영어에서는 _____/_____/일/_____ 순서로 나타낸다.

(3) **전화 번호:** 하나씩 _____로 읽는다.

(4) **돈, 화폐:** 숫자와 함께 _____ 단위를 붙여서 읽는다.

(5) **소수점:** 소수점까지는 _____로 읽고 소수점은 _____로 읽는다. 소수점 이하는 기수로 하나씩 읽는다.

(6) **분수:** 분자는 _____로 읽고, 분모는 _____로 읽는다. 분자가 2 이상이면 분모는 _____으로 읽는다.

다음 숫자 읽기에서 틀린 부분을 바르게 고쳐 다시 쓰세요.

1 1984년: nineteen eight-four

→ _____

2 $\frac{3}{4}$: three fourth

→ _____

3 ☎ 246–2103: two hundred forty-six two one o three

→ _____

4 35.99: thirty-five point ninety-nine

→ _____

5 $79.78: seventy-nine dollar seventy-eight cent

→ _____

6 10월 24일: October two four

→ _____

7 1728년: one seven two eight

→ _____

8 2000년 3월 16일: two thousand, March sixteenth

→ _____

9 ☎ (02) 147–3215: area code zero second, one four seven three two one five

→ _____

10 ₩2,250: two thousandth, two hundredth fiftieth won

→ _____

다음 문장에서 틀린 부분을 바르게 고쳐 다시 쓰세요.

1 It is Jennifer's eight novel.

→ _____

2 They live on the fifteen floor.

→ _____

3 She is twelfth years old.

→ _____

4 This is a building of forty-fifth stories.

→ _____

5 The five day of the week is Thursday.

→ _____

6 There are thirtieth people on the playground.

→ _____

7 Here is the four station from the gallery.

→ _____

8 The three question is very difficult.

→ _____

9 The bank is the seven building on your right.

→ _____

10 Judy sends tenth letters to her friends.

→ _____

novel 소설
playground 운동장
station 역
gallery 미술관
bank 은행
letter 편지

다음 우리말과 같도록 빈칸에 알맞은 말을 쓰세요.

1 Brian과 John은 5학년이다.

→ Brian and John are in the _____ grade.

2 Mark의 사무실은 12층에 있다.

→ Mark's office is on the _____ floor.

3 이 약은 식사 후 30분에 드세요.

→ Take this medicine _____ minutes after a meal.

4 이번이 나의 2번째 일본여행이다.

→ This is my _____ trip to Japan.

5 내일은 중학교에서의 첫 날이다.

→ Tomorrow is the _____ day of the middle school.

6 내 생일은 10월 31일이다.

→ My birthday is on _____ thirty-first.

7 이것은 저것보다 2배 더 크다.

→ This is _____ as large as that.

8 Karen은 그 줄에서 10번째 학생이다.

→ Karen is the _____ student in the line.

9 그 이야기는 2가지의 다른 결말이 있다.

→ There are _____ different endings of the story.

10 그녀의 전화번호는 123-4561번이다.

→ Her phone number is ____ ____ ____ four five six one.

---

medicine 약

trip 여행

tomorrow 내일

middle school 중학교

different 다른

ending 결말

 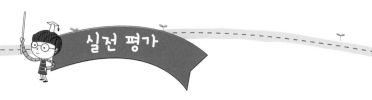

1 다음 중 성격이 다른 것을 고르세요.

① first
② eighteen
③ eleventh
④ twentieth

[2～3] 다음 기수와 서수의 관계가 바르지 않은 것을 고르세요.

2
① five – fifth
② nine – ninth
③ twelve – twelveth
④ thirty – thirtieth

3
① three – third
② seven – seventh
③ fourteen – fourteenth
④ one hundred – first hundred

4 다음 숫자를 기수와 서수로 잘못 표기한 것을 고르세요.

① 2 : two – twoth
② 6 : six – sixth
③ 8 : eight – eighth
④ 15 : fifteen – fifteenth

5 다음 우리말에 맞게 빈칸에 알맞은 말을 쓰세요.

> 회원의 $\frac{3}{5}$ 이상이 그 모임에 참석한다.

→ More than _____ of the members attend the meeting.

[6～7] 다음 중 숫자를 영어로 잘못 나타낸 것을 고르세요.

6
① 3.18 = three point one eight
② 3,261 = three thousand, two hundred sixty-one
③ $\frac{3}{7}$ = three seventh
④ $52.43 = fifty-two dollars forty-three cents

7
① 4월 5일 = the fifth of April
② ₩570 = five hundred and seventy wons
③ $\frac{1}{4}$ = one quarter
④ 91.25 = ninety-one point two five

8 다음 중 연도를 읽은 표현이 올바른 것을 고르세요.

① 1978년 = nineteen seventy-eight
② 1999년 = nineteen ninety-ninth
③ 1234년 = one thousand, two hundred thirty-four
④ 845년 = eight four five

[9～10] 다음 중 올바르지 않은 문장을 고르세요.

9
① I have fifty dollars.
② They buy five apples.
③ I am eleven years old.
④ The boy is two in this line.

10 ① He collects nine stamps.

② The restaurant is on the fifth floor.

③ This is two as large as that.

④ My sister is in the sixth grade.

[11~12] 다음 전화번호를 영어로 쓰세요.

11 ☎ 375-2148

→ _____

12 ☎ (02) 862-9307

→ _____

13 다음 표현이 나타내는 숫자를 고르세요.

two and a half

① $\frac{1}{2}$ ② $2\frac{1}{2}$

③ $\frac{1}{3}$ ④ $\frac{2}{3}$

[14~16] 다음 중 올바른 문장을 고르세요.

14 ① This is his four book.

② Push the first button.

③ There are third bedroom.

④ Alice has seventh dogs.

15 ① It is Ashley's eleven album.

② She sends tenth letters to him.

③ There are forty people in the park.

④ The two day of the week is Monday.

16 ① Here is the three station from the bank.

② This is a building of sixty-third stories.

③ She gives one hundredth dollars to him.

④ This is my second trip to Korea.

17 다음 배수를 영어로 쓰세요.

3배 → _____

18 다음 날짜를 영어로 읽을 때, 빈칸에 알맞은 말을 쓰세요.

1969년 6월 15일

→ the _____ of _____

_____

[19~20] 다음 우리말과 같도록 어색한 부분을 고쳐 다시 쓰세요.

19

7번째 문제는 매우 쉽다.

The seven question is very easy.

→ _____

20

나는 런던에서 8년 동안 살고 있다.

I live in London for eighth years.

→ _____

 서술형 평가

A Tony가 친구들과 줄다리기를 하기 위해 줄을 서 있습니다. 그림을 보고, 빈칸에 알맞은 순서를 영어로 쓰세요.

fourth

eleventh

ninth

seventh

second

B 다음 〈보기〉에서 알맞은 것을 골라 쓰세요.

〈보기〉 one third   a quarter   a half   three fourths

$\dfrac{1}{4}$ $\dfrac{1}{2}$ $\dfrac{3}{4}$ $\dfrac{1}{3}$

1 _____   **2** _____   **3** _____   **4** _____

C 다음 괄호 안의 숫자를 기수 또는 서수로 알맞게 고쳐 쓰세요.

1 My house is on the _____ floor. (7)

2 The building has _____ offices. (15)

3 The _____ month of the year is January. (1)

Unit 2

부정대명사, 재귀대명사

부정대명사의 의미와 쓰임을 이해하고 활용할 수 있다.

재귀대명사의 의미와 쓰임을 이해하고 활용할 수 있다.

부정대명사와 재귀대명사를 문장을 통해 표현할 수 있다.

정해지지 않은 사람, 사물 또는 그 수량을 막연하게 가리킬 때 부정대명사를 사용해요.

부정대명사는 부정확한 것을 가리킨다고 해서 부정대명사라고 해요.

재귀대명사는 <주어 자신>을 가리키는 말로 인칭대명사에 -self(복수형은 -selves)를

붙여서 만들어요.

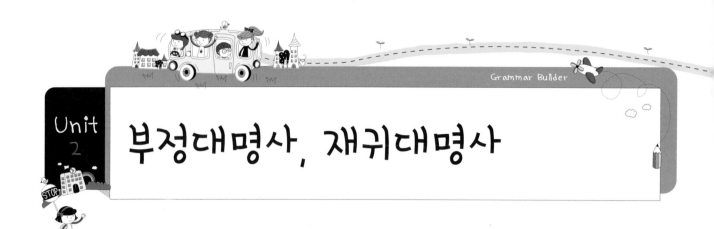

Unit 2

부정대명사, 재귀대명사

1. 부정대명사의 의미

부정대명사는 정해져 있지 않은 사람이나 사물 또는 그 수량을 막연하게 가리킬 때 쓴다. 대표적인 것에는 one이 있다.

→ one, some, any, all, each, both, other, another

2. one, ones, one's

(1) 앞에 나온 명사와 같은 종류이지만 불특정한 것을 나타낼 때 쓴다.

• 복수형은 ones이고 소유격은 one's이다.

• 앞에 이미 언급된 특정 대상은 대명사 it으로 쓴다.

I need a pencil. Do you have one? 나는 연필이 필요하다. 너 하나 있니?

> ＊one과 it을 구별하는 방법
> • 앞에서 언급한 물건과 같은 종류의 것 → 부정대명사 one
> • 앞에서 언급한 바로 그 물건 → 대명사 it
> My dad gave me a pencil. But I lost it. (it = the pencil)
> 나의 아빠가 나에게 연필을 주셨다. 그러나 나는 그것을 잃어버렸다.

(2) 일반적인 사람을 나타낼 때 사용한다.

One should keep one's promise. (One＝We) 사람들은 약속을 지켜야 한다.

3. some, any

some과 any는 '몇 개, 얼마, 어느 정도'라는 부정확한 수량을 나타낸다.

> - some은 긍정문에, any는 부정문과 의문문에 쓰인다.
> - some[any] of + 셀 수 있는 명사의 복수형 → 복수 취급
> - some[any] of + 셀 수 없는 명사 → 단수 취급

Some of the books are interesting. 그 책들 중 몇 권은 재미있다.

Some of the ice is cracked. 그 얼음 중 일부는 금이 갔다.

I don't want any of these. 나는 이것들의 일부를 원하지 않는다.

> **Pop Quiz**   Ⅰ. 다음 괄호 안에서 알맞은 것을 고르세요.
>
> · I don't have an eraser. Can I borrow (one, it)?

4. each, both, all

each는 '각각'이고 both는 '둘 다'이며 all은 '모두'이다.

> - each는 대명사와 형용사로 쓰인다. → 단수 취급
> - both는 대명사와 형용사로 쓰인다. → 복수 취급
> - all은 대명사와 형용사로 쓰인다. → 사람이면 복수, 사물이면 단수 취급

Each of the girls has a doll. 그 소녀들은 각각 인형을 가지고 있다. (→ Each girl)

Both of the boys are happy. 그 소년들은 둘 다 모두 행복하다. (→ Both boys)

All (of) the students eat pizza. 모든 학생들이 피자를 먹는다.

Every boy is very tall. 모든 소년은 매우 키가 크다. (every + 단수명사)

every는 '모든 ~'이라는 뜻으로 단독으로 쓰일 수 없으며, 그 다음에 반드시 단수 명사가 온다. → 단수 취급

5. other, another

other는 '다른 것(사람)'의 뜻으로 사람이나 사물에 모두 쓰이며, another는 '또 다른 하나'라는 뜻으로 단수 취급한다.

> • one ~ the other …: (둘 중) 하나는 ~이고 나머지 하나는 …
> • some ~ others …: 몇몇은 ~이고 나머지는 …
> • one ~ another … the other …: (셋 중) 하나는 ~ 또 하나는 … 나머지는 …

I have another question. 나는 질문이 하나 더 있다.

He has two sons. One is a teacher and the other is a doctor.

그는 아들이 둘 있다. 하나는 선생님이고 다른 하나는 의사이다.

She has three pets. One is a dog, another is a cat, and the other is a turtle.

그녀는 애완동물이 셋 있다. 하나는 개, 다른 하나는 고양이, 나머지는 거북이이다.

1, 2인칭은 소유격에 self(selves)를 붙이고 3인칭은 목적격에 self(selves)를 붙인다.

6. 재귀대명사

재귀대명사는 주어 자신을 가리키는 말로 인칭대명사에 -self(복수형은 -selves)가 붙어서 '~ 자신'이라는 뜻이다.

She is looking at herself in the mirror.
그녀는 거울로 그녀 자신을 보고 있다.

	단수	복수
1인칭	myself 나 자신	ourselves 우리 자신
2인칭	yourself 당신 자신	yourselves 당신들 자신
3인칭	himself 그 자신 herself 그녀 자신 itself 그것 자체	themselves 그들 자신

> **Pop Quiz**　2. 다음 괄호 안에서 알맞은 것을 고르세요.
>
> (Both, Each) of her brothers are studying in Japan.

다음 괄호 안에서 알맞은 것을 골라 동그라미 하세요.

1 I don't have an eraser. Please lend me (it, one).

2 This pencil is nice. I like (it, one).

3 (Some, Any) of them are late.

4 I need some notebooks. Do you have (some, any)?

5 (Each, Both) of the boys has his own room.

6 (Each, Both) of them have talents for art.

7 He doesn't like (some, any) of the dogs.

8 (All, Every) of them have dinner together.

9 (Each, All) of the students has a computer.

10 (All, Every) the children have their own bike.

11 (Every, All) girl likes pretty dolls.

12 (One, It) should do one's best.

13 I want a new radio. Show me (one, it).

14 (Both, Each) of the students are hungry.

15 I lost my watch. I have to buy (one, it).

16 (All, Every) of them are running after a rabbit.

lend 빌려주다
own 자신의
talent 재주, 재능
run after 쫓다
have to ~해야 한다

다음 괄호 안에서 알맞은 것을 골라 동그라미 하세요.

greedy 욕심 많은
diligent 근면한
useful 유용한
furniture 가구
newspaper 신문
different 다른

1 Every man (is, are) greedy.

2 Some of the tables (is, are) old.

3 Each of us (know, knows) Ashley.

4 All of the men (is, are) very diligent.

5 Every man and woman (like, likes) the student.

6 All the boys (is, are) waiting in a line.

7 Each (student, students) in the class is kind.

8 Every (photo, photos) is great.

9 Some of the books (is, are) very useful.

10 (Each, Every) of them is from a different country.

11 (All, Every) house on the street has a blue roof.

12 Some of the furniture (is, are) too expensive.

13 There are six books. Some are mine, (another, others) are hers.

14 I want today's newspaper. This is an old (one, it).

15 She has two hats. One is red, and (any, the other) is pink.

16 He has three dogs. One is Happy, (another, some) is Love, and the (other, others) is Smart.

다음 괄호 안에서 알맞은 것을 골라 동그라미 하세요.

mirror 거울
fault 잘못
blame 비난하다
paint 칠하다
proud 자랑스러운

1 He makes (me, myself) delicious pizza.

2 Alice cuts (her, herself) with a knife.

3 My brother looks at (him, himself) in the mirror.

4 Mr. Smith teaches (us, ourselves) English.

5 It is not your fault. Don't blame (you, yourself).

6 She draws the picture (her, herself).

7 The little boys are proud of (their, themselves).

8 Bill makes this book (his, himself).

9 Heaven helps those who help (them, themselves).

10 He asks (her, herself) some questions.

11 Adam gives (her, herself) a ring.

12 Mark paints the wall (him, himself).

13 The artist shows (me, myself) the paintings.

14 She talks about (her, herself).

15 I say to (me, myself), "I am happy."

16 We have a good vacation. We enjoy (us, ourselves).

다음 괄호 안에서 알맞은 것을 골라 동그라미 하세요.

stamp 우표
borrow 빌리다
hide 숨기다
blond 금발의
only 단지
flag 기, 깃발

1 I need some stamps. Do you have (some, any)?

2 I don't have a ruler. Can I borrow (one, it)?

3 (Any, Some) of the books are in my room.

4 The kids hide (them, themselves) under the table.

5 (Each, Both) of my parents are doctors.

6 (Each, Both) of boys has a red pen.

7 Give me three red pencils and two blue (one, ones).

8 I see a cute dog. (One, It) is black and white.

9 (Every, All) girl has short blond hair.

10 Each boy (have, has) his own computer.

11 He only thinks about (him, himself).

12 She talks about (him, himself) to people.

13 Each of the children (have, has) a robot.

14 Every (country, countries) has a national flag.

15 Do you have any balls? – No, I don't have (some, any).

16 I have two pets. (One, Another) is a cat, and (another, the other) is a dog.

다음 빈칸에 들어갈 말을 〈보기〉에서 골라 쓰세요.

ask 질문하다

carry 운반하다

among ~의 사이에

〈보기〉 one   it   some   any   another

I Many students are here. But _____ are late.
일부

2 I make a card and give _____ to Peter.
그것

3 I need a soccer ball. I have to buy a new _____.
–것

4 I don't like this toy car. Show me _____.
다른 것

5 I have many candies. I don't want _____ of these.
일부

6 Do you have a cat? – Yes, I have _____.
–것

7 _____ of the movies are interesting.
몇몇

8 _____ student in the class asks the question.
다른 한 명의

9 He is carring a box. _____ looks heavy.
그것

10 _____ of them read the *Harry Potter* series.
일부

II Among them, I like the green _____.
–것

12 I want some flowers. Do you have _____?
조금(일부)

다음 빈칸에 들어갈 말을 〈보기〉에서 골라 쓰세요.

〈보기〉 each   both   all   every   another   other   others

empty 빈
bat 야구방망이
hall 강당
prepare 준비하다
silent 조용한
purse 지갑

1 _____ of these seats are empty.
　　모두

2 _____ of the girls has her own room.
　　각각

3 We buy two bats. One is $10, and the _____ is $13.
　　　　　　　　　　　　　　　　　　　다른 하나

4 _____ man in the city is waiting for her.
　　모든

5 _____ of the women in the hall are singing.
　　둘 다

6 _____ the boys prepare for the exam.
　　모두

7 _____ student has a name tag.
　　각각의

8 This shirt is too big on me. I'll try on _____.
　　　　　　　　　　　　　　　　　다른 것

9 _____ of the boy and the girl are silent.
　　둘 다

10 _____ man in the restaurant wears the hat.
　　모든

11 He has two purses. One is big, and the _____ is small.
　　　　　　　　　　　　　　　　　다른 하나

12 There are many flowers in the garden. Some are white,
　　and _____ are yellow.
　　　　다른 일부

Step 2 — Build Up 1

다음 우리말과 같도록 빈칸에 알맞은 말을 쓰세요.

1 _____ are green, and _____ are orange.

어떤 것들은 초록색이고 다른 것들은 주황색이다.

2 This pencil isn't good. Show me _____.

이 연필은 좋지 않아요. 다른 것을 보여주세요.

3 _____ of the students get up early everyday.

그 학생들의 몇몇은 매일 일찍 일어난다.

4 _____ girl has this hairpin.

모든 소녀들은 이 헤어핀을 가지고 있다.

5 My computer is not working. I have to buy _____.

나의 컴퓨터는 작동하지 않는다. 나는 하나를 사야 한다.

6 _____ of the boys are thirsty.

소년은 둘 다 목이 마르다.

7 _____ the students in the class like the movie.

교실에 있는 모든 학생들은 그 영화를 좋아한다.

8 _____ girl likes a handsome singer.

각각의 소녀들은 잘생긴 가수를 좋아한다.

9 They have two sons. _____ is a lawyer and _____ is a soldier.

그들은 아들이 두 명이다. 한 명은 변호사이고 다른 한 명은 군인이다.

10 I have three pieces of furniture. _____ is a desk, _____ is a bed, and _____ is a table.

나는 가구 세 점을 가지고 있다. 하나는 책상이고, 다른 하나는 침대이며, 나머지 하나는 탁자이다.

work 작동하다
lawyer 변호사

부정대명사, 재귀대명사 · **43**

다음 우리말과 같도록 빈칸에 알맞은 말을 쓰세요.

star 인기 배우
information 정보
letter 편지

1 _____ woman likes the movie star.

모든 여성이 그 영화배우를 좋아한다.

2 _____ of them knows Jacob.

그들은 각각 Jacob을 알고 있다.

3 I say to _____, "I am OK."

나는 나 자신에게 "나는 괜찮아."라고 말한다.

4 These are Ann and Sue. _____ of them are eleven.

이 사람들은 Ann과 Sue이다. 그들 둘 다 11살이다.

5 I don't like this skirt. Can you show me _____?

이 치마가 마음에 들지 않아요. 다른 것을 보여주실래요?

6 Don't buy these pants. Buy those _____.

이 바지를 사지 마라. 저것을 사라.

7 _____ of the information is very useful.

그 정보의 일부는 매우 유용하다.

8 _____ of the houses in this town are clean.

이 마을에 있는 모든 집들은 깨끗하다.

9 There are six letters. _____ is mine, and _____ are his.

6통의 편지가 있다. 하나는 나의 것이고 나머지들은 그의 것이다.

10 I have three brothers. _____ is Brian, _____ is Matt, and _____ is Mark.

나는 3명의 형이 있다. 한 명은 Brian이고, 다른 한 명은 Matt이며, 나머지는 Mark이다.

다음 인칭대명사의 재귀대명사를 쓰세요.

1 he _____ 2 it _____

3 you(복수) _____ 4 I _____

5 they _____ 6 you(단수) _____

7 she _____ 8 we _____

introduce 소개하다
neighbor 이웃
ride 타다
believe 믿다

다음 우리말과 같도록 빈칸에 알맞은 말을 쓰세요.

9 나는 새 이웃에게 나 자신을 소개한다.

→ I introduce _____ to my new neighbor.

10 너는 오직 너 자신만 생각한다.

→ You only think about _____.

11 그 소녀는 스스로 자전거를 탄다.

→ The girl rides the bike _____.

12 너희들은 너희들 자신을 믿는 게 필요하다.

→ You need to believe in _____.

13 그들은 이 맛있는 피자를 직접 만든다.

→ They make this delicious pizza _____.

14 Peter는 가끔 거울 속의 그에게 이야기를 한다.

→ Peter sometimes talks to _____ in the mirror.

15 그 학생들은 파티에서 마음껏 즐긴다.

→ The students enjoy _____ at the party.

다음 빈칸에 알맞은 말을 쓰세요.

1 one, ones, one's

one은 앞에 나온 명사와 같은 종류이지만 불특정한 것을 나타낼 때 쓴다.

• 복수형은 _____이고 소유격은 _____이다.

• 앞에서 언급한 물건과 같은 종류의 것 → 부정대명사 _____

• 앞에서 언급한 바로 그 물건 → 대명사 _____

2 some, any

some과 any는 '몇 개, 얼마, 어느 정도'라는 부정확한 수량을 나타낸다.

• _____은 긍정문에, _____는 부정문과 의문문에 쓰인다.

• some[any] of 셀 수 있는 명사의 복수형 → _____ 취급

• some[any] of 셀 수 없는 명사 → _____ 취급

3 each, both, all

each는 '각각'이고 both는 '둘 다'이며 all은 '모두'이다.

• each는 대명사와 형용사로 쓰인다. → _____ 취급

• both는 대명사와 형용사로 쓰인다. → _____ 취급

• all은 대명사와 형용사로 쓰인다. → _____이면 복수, 사물이면 _____ 취급

• every는 '모든 ~'이라는 뜻으로 그 뒤에 _____명사가 온다. → _____ 취급

4 other, another

• one ~ the _____ ...: (둘 중) 하나는 ~이고 나머지 하나는 …

• some ~ _____ ...: 몇몇은 ~이고 나머지는 …

• one ~ _____ ... the _____ ...: 하나는 ~ 또 하나는 … 나머지는 …

5 재귀대명사

재귀대명사는 주어 자신을 가리키는 말로 인칭대명사에 -_____(복수형은 -_____)가 붙어서 '~ 자신'이라는 뜻이다.

다음 문장에서 밑줄 친 부분을 바르게 고쳐 쓰세요.

1 Each of the boys <u>have</u> his own chair. → _____

2 All the students <u>is</u> very kind. → _____

3 Let me introduce <u>me</u>. I'm Billy. → _____

4 We travel <u>any</u> countries in Europe. → _____

5 Every <u>men</u> is waiting for him. → _____

6 I don't like this hairpin. Show me <u>one</u>. → _____

7 I have two dolls. One is small, and
<u>another</u> is big. → _____

8 All the <u>bag</u> on the table are heavy. → _____

9 I make pizza for <u>me</u>. → _____

10 <u>Any</u> of his friends have a tent. → _____

11 There are many books. Some are novels,
and <u>anothers</u> are comic books. → _____

12 They enjoy <u>them</u> at the party. → _____

13 Every girl in the class <u>are</u> outgoing. → _____

14 Both of his <u>book</u> are very thick. → _____

15 We have three friends. One is Judy,
<u>some</u> is Sophie, and the other is Amy. → _____

travel 여행하다
novel 소설
outgoing 사교적인
thick 두꺼운

다음 문장에서 밑줄 친 부분을 바르게 고쳐 쓰세요.

move 움직이다
drop 떨어지다
protect 보호하다
quiet 조용한
confident 자신이 있는
noodle 국수

1 The box is too heavy. Can you move <u>one</u>?

→ _____

2 Some of the water <u>are</u> dropping. → _____

3 All of the <u>boy</u> are playing soccer. → _____

4 Both of the men <u>is</u> waiting for the train. → _____

5 We must protect <u>us</u> from the enemies. → _____

6 Every <u>men</u> knows the famous singer. → _____

7 There are many flowers in the shop.
Some are roses, and <u>other</u> are lilies. → _____

8 Each of the <u>woman</u> plays the piano. → _____

9 <u>All</u> student has to be quiet in class. → _____

10 You should take care of <u>you</u>. → _____

11 I have two dog. <u>Another</u> is a Jindo dog
and the other is a poodle. → _____

12 <u>Any</u> of the buildings are very big. → _____

13 Juliet is confident in <u>her</u>. → _____

14 Each <u>men</u> has his own problem. → _____

15 She prepares three foods. One is noodle, another
is pizza, and the <u>others</u> is rice. → _____

다음 우리말과 같도록 주어진 말을 참고하여 영어로 쓰세요.

empty 빈, 비어 있는
promise 약속

1 모든 학생은 이 책을 가지고 있다. (every, have, this)

→ _____

2 그 소년들은 각각 피자를 먹는다. (each of, eat, pizza)

→ _____

3 그 소녀들은 모두 키가 매우 크다. (all of, tall, very)

→ _____

4 그 방들의 일부는 비워 있다. (some of, empty, rooms)

→ _____

5 사람들은 약속을 지켜야 한다. (one, one's, should, keep)

→ _____

6 나는 약간의 쿠키를 원한다. 너는 약간 갖고 있니? (some, cookies, any)

→ _____

7 그 남자들 둘은 다 컴퓨터 게임을 한다. (both of, the men, play)

→ _____

8 일부는 개를 좋아하고, 다른 일부는 고양이를 좋아한다. (some, others)

→ _____

9 5권의 책이 있다. 하나는 나의 것이고 나머지들은 그의 것이다. (one, others)

→ There are five books. _____

10 나는 가방이 2개 있다. 하나는 분홍색이고 다른 하나는 초록색이다. (one, other)

→ I have two bags. _____

[1~2] 다음 중 빈칸에 알맞은 것을 고르세요.

1

> A: Do you have a fork?
> B: Yes, I have _____.

① it   ② one
③ some   ④ any

2

> There are two little bags on the table.
> One is green and _____ is blue.

① other   ② others
③ the other   ④ another

3 우리말과 같은 뜻이 되도록 빈칸에 알맞은 말을 고르세요.

> 이 책들 중 몇 권은 재미있지만, 몇 권은 그렇지 않다.
> = Some of these books are interesting, but _____ are not.

① other   ② the other
③ others   ④ the others

4 다음 중 밑줄 친 부분의 쓰임이 잘못된 것을 고르세요.

① They do it themselves.
② I see the man myself.
③ She looks at herself in the mirror.
④ He makes yourself doughnuts.

[5~6] 다음 두 문장의 의미가 같도록 빈칸에 알맞은 말을 쓰세요.

5 All of the items have price tags.
= _____ of the items has a price tag.

6 The students have fun at the party.
= The students enjoy _____ at the party.

[7~8] 다음 빈칸에 들어갈 말이 바르게 짝지어진 것을 고르세요.

7

> There are many people in the restaurant. _____ are eating pizza, and _____ are eating spaghetti.

① Some, others
② Some, some
③ Some, the other
④ Others, others

8

> Peter draws three shapes. One is a circle, _____ is a triangle, and _____ is a square.

① another, the other
② another, the others
③ the other, another
④ the other, the others

9 다음 중 빈칸에 공통으로 들어갈 알맞은 말을 고르세요.

> · He is proud of _____.
> · Brian makes this bread _____.

① him   ② himself
③ her   ④ herself

[10~11] 다음 대화의 빈칸에 들어갈 알맞은 말을 쓰세요.

10 A: I don't have coins. Do you have any coins?
B: No, I don't have _____.

11 A: Do you make the box?
B: Yes. I make it _____.

12 다음 밑줄 친 부분이 가리키는 것을 영어로 쓰세요.

> I have an old computer, but my big brother has a new <u>one</u>.

→ _____

13 다음 문장과 뜻이 같도록 빈칸에 알맞은 말을 쓰세요.

> All the cities have the same problem.
> = Every _____ _____ the same problem.

_____ _____

[14~16] 다음 중 알맞은 문장을 고르세요.

14 ① Both of his cups are clean.
② Each teams have five players.
③ All the boys swims well.
④ Every teachers have their own chair.

15 ① Every students need friends.
② Any of them are wrong.
③ Each of the girls has a hairpin.
④ Both of them is making salad.

16 ① Her idea is a good it.
② This skirt is short. I don't wear it.
③ Those pants are expensive. I want cheap them.
④ My umbrella is broken. I need to fix one.

17 다음 밑줄 친 부분 중 어색한 것을 고르세요.
Which do you like best of ① <u>these</u> three bags? ② <u>One</u> is white,
③ <u>another</u> is black, and ④ <u>the others</u> is orange.

[18~19] 다음 우리말과 같도록 빈칸에 알맞은 말을 쓰세요.

18 그 소년들은 둘 다 대답을 알고 있다.
→ _____ of the boys know the answer.

19 Alice가 직접 너의 개를 돌보고 있다.
→ Alice takes care of your dog _____.

A 다음 우리말과 같도록 빈칸에 알맞은 말을 쓰세요.

1 우리 감자 좀 있어? = Do we have _____ potatoes?

2 응, 냉장고에 좀 있어. = Yes, there are _____ in the refrigerator.

B 다음 그림을 보고, 알맞은 말을 골라 문장을 완성하세요.

❶ 　　❷ 　　❸

〈보기〉 each　　both　　all

1 _____ of these _____ are mine. (toy)

2 _____ of my _____ wear glasses. (parent)

3 _____ of the _____ has a ribbon on it. (box)

C 다음 표를 보고, 재귀대명사를 이용하여 빈칸에 알맞은 말을 쓰세요.

Question	Peter	Sally	Dan
자기 자신을 믿습니까?	Yes (○) / No ( )	Yes ( ) / No (×)	Yes (○) / No ( )
스스로에 대해 자랑스럽게 느낍니까?	Yes (○) / No ( )	Yes ( ) / No (×)	Yes (○) / No ( )

1 Peter believes in _____. But Sally doesn't believe in _____.

2 Peter and Dan are proud of _____.

비교 구문

비교급의 의미와 쓰임을 이해하고 활용할 수 있다.

비교급과 최상급을 만드는 방법을 이해할 수 있다.

비교급과 최상급을 문장 속에서 이해하고 활용할 수 있다.

형용사나 부사를 이용해 비교 대상이 둘일 때에는 비교급을 말하며 비교 대상이 셋 이상일 때에는 최상급으로 표현해요. 또한 형용사나 부사의 원급이란 원래의 형용사나 부사의 형태로 -er이나 -est가 붙지 않은 상태를 말해요.

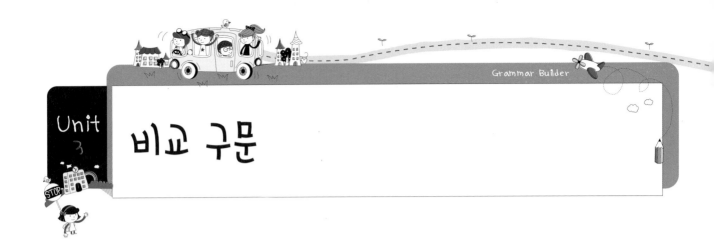

Unit
3

비교 구문

1. 비교급과 최상급의 의미

형용사나 부사를 이용해 비교 대상이 둘일 때는 '~보다 더 크다'처럼 비교급으로 말하며, 비교
대상이 셋 이상일 때는 '~중에서 가장 …하다'처럼 최상급으로 표현한다.

My brother is tall. 나의 남동생은 키가 크다. [원급]

Matt is taller **than Kate.** Matt는 Kate보다 키가 더 크다. [비교급]

Tom is the tallest **of the three.** Tom은 셋 중에서 키가 가장 크다. [최상급]

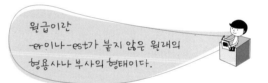

원급이란
-er이나 -est가 붙지 않은 원래의
형용사나 부사의 형태이다.

2. 비교급, 최상급 만드는 법

대부분의 형용사나 부사는 원급에 -er을 붙여 비교급을, -est를 붙여 최상급을 만든다.

(1) 규칙 변화

	비교급(최상급)	원급	비교급(더 ~한)	최상급(가장 ~한)
대부분의 형용사, 부사	+ -er[-est]	tall 키가 큰	taller	tallest
		fast 빨리	faster	fastest
		old 늙은	older	oldest
-e로 끝나는 형용사, 부사	+ -r[-st]	large 큰	larger	largest
		cute 귀여운	cuter	cutest
		wise 현명한	wiser	wisest

	비교급(최상급)	원급	비교급(더 ~한)	최상급(가장 ~한)
모음 1개 +자음 1개로 끝나는 형용사, 부사	마지막 자음 +-er[-est]	hot 뜨거운 big 큰 fat 뚱뚱한	hotter bigger fatter	hottest biggest fattest
-y로 끝나는 형용사, 부사	y를 i로 바꾸고, -er[-est]	happy 행복한 easy 쉬운 busy 바쁜	happier easier busier	happiest easiest busiest
3음절 이상 형용사, 부사	more[most] +형용사, 부사	beautiful 아름다운 popular 인기 있는 interesting 재미있는	more beautiful more popular more interesting	most beautiful most popular most interesting

(2) 불규칙 변화

원급	비교급	최상급
good, well 좋은, 잘	better	best
bad, ill 나쁜	worse	worst
many, much 많은	more	most
little 작은, 적은	less	least

Pop Quiz

1. 다음 단어의 비교급, 최상급을 쓰세요.
❶ small – _____ – _____
❷ big – _____ – _____

3. 원급과 비교급을 이용한 비교

(1) as 원급 as: ~만큼 …하다

주어+동사	as 원급 as	비교 대상

Judy is as tall as John. Judy는 John만큼 키가 크다.

Judy is not as tall as Eric. Judy는 Eric만큼 키가 크지 않다. (= Eric is taller than Judy.)

(2) 비교급+than: ~보다 더 …한

주어+동사	비교급 than	비교 대상

The elephant is bigger than the horse. 코끼리는 말보다 더 크다.

Dan runs faster than Peter. Dan은 Peter보다 더 빨리 달린다.

4. 최상급을 이용한 비교

형용사의 최상급 앞에는 항상 the가 들어가며 in이나 of를 사용하여 비교 범위나 비교 대상을 쓴다. 부사의 최상급 앞에는 the가 붙지 않는다.

주어+동사	the 최상급(+명사)	in+비교 범위 of+비교 대상

He is the youngest boy in the town. 그는 그 마을에서 가장 어린 소년이다.

She is the tallest woman of the five. 그녀는 다섯 중에 가장 큰 여자이다.

Tony studies hardest of all. Tony는 모두 중에서 가장 열심히 공부한다. [부사]

> **Pop Quiz** 2. 다음 괄호 안에서 알맞은 것을 고르세요.
> ❶ She is taller (as, than) I. ❷ He is the tallest (in, of) the six.

다음 괄호 안에서 비교급과 최상급을 골라 동그라미 하세요.

1 thin – (thiner, thinner) – (thinest, thinnest)

2 little – (littler, less) – (littlest, least)

3 short – (shorter, shortter) – (shortest, shorttest)

4 big – (biger, bigger) – (bigest, biggest)

5 large – (larger, largeer) – (largest, largeest)

6 difficult – (difficulter, more difficult) –
   (difficultest, most difficult)

7 much – (mucher, more) – (muchest, most)

8 old – (older, more old) – (oldest, most old)

9 pretty – (prettyer, prettier) – (prettyest, prettiest)

10 dark – (darker, darkier) – (darkest, darkiest)

11 cheap – (cheaper, cheapper) – (cheapest, cheappest)

12 beautiful – (beautifuler, more beautiful) –
   (beautifulest, most beautiful)

13 fast – (faster, fastter) – (fastest, fasttest)

14 ill – (iller, worse) – (illest, worst)

15 long – (longer, longger) – (longest, longgest)

16 heavy – (heavyer, heavier) – (heavyest, heaviest)

thin 얇은, 가는
dark 어두운
cheap 싼
ill 나쁜
heavy 무거운

다음 괄호 안에서 비교급과 최상급을 골라 동그라미 하세요.

1   busy – (busyer, busier) – (busyest, busiest)

2   young – (younger, youngger) – (youngest, younggest)

3   happy – (happyer, happier) – (happyest, happiest)

4   hot – (hoter, hotter) – (hotest, hottest)

5   nice – (nicer, niceer) – (nicest, niceest)

6   easy – (easyer, easier) – (easyest, easiest)

7   famous – (famouser, more famous) –
    (famousest, most famous)

8   small – (smaller, smallr) – (smallest, smallst)

9   well – (weller, better) – (wellest, best)

10   bad – (bader, worse) – (badest, worst)

11   many – (more many, more) – (most many, most)

12   popular – (popularer, more popular) –
    (popularest, most popular)

13   wise – (wiser, more wise) – (wisest, more wise)

14   good – (better, gooder) – (best, goodest)

15   tall – (tallier, taller) – (talliest, tallest)

16   fat – (fatter, fater) – (fattest, fatest)

busy 바쁜
hot 더운
popular 유명한
wise 현명한
fat 뚱뚱한

다음 형용사나 부사의 비교급과 최상급을 쓰세요.

1 many – _____ – _____

2 special – _____ – _____

3 easy – _____ – _____

4 strange – _____ – _____

5 happy – _____ – _____

6 popular – _____ – _____

7 fast – _____ – _____

8 dry – _____ – _____

9 strong – _____ – _____

10 lovely – _____ – _____

11 bad – _____ – _____

12 high – _____ – _____

13 big – _____ – _____

14 little – _____ – _____

15 short – _____ – _____

16 careful – _____ – _____

special 특별한
strange 이상한
dry 마른
lovely 사랑스러운
careful 조심스러운

Step 1

Check Up 4

다음 형용사나 부사의 비교급과 최상급을 쓰세요.

dangerous 위험한
useful 유용한
polite 예의 바른
wet 젖은

1 hungry – _____ – _____

2 well – _____ – _____

3 dangerous – _____ – _____

4 hot – _____ – _____

5 useful – _____ – _____

6 pretty – _____ – _____

7 much – _____ – _____

8 smart – _____ – _____

9 polite – _____ – _____

10 large – _____ – _____

11 wet – _____ – _____

12 cute – _____ – _____

13 handsome – _____ – _____

14 thin – _____ – _____

15 angry – _____ – _____

16 cheap – _____ – _____

다음 단어를 활용하여 비교급 또는 최상급 문장을 완성하세요.

get up 일어나다

early 일찍

brave 용감한

1 A tiger is the _____ animal in the zoo. (strong)

2 Brian is _____ than Julia. (smart)

3 He is the _____ student of his friends. (busy)

4 Sue runs _____ than Mark. (fast)

5 I get up _____ than my sister. (early)

6 My mom is _____ than my dad. (young)

7 You are _____ than them. (happy)

8 This bag is _____ than that one. (heavy)

9 Your puppy is the _____ of the five. (cute)

10 You are the _____ mother in the world. (good)

11 The star looks _____ than the others. (dark)

12 He is the _____ man in our town. (brave)

13 He is more _____ than his brother. (famous)

14 I like math _____ than science. (much)

15 This building is the _____ in this city. (big)

16 Music is more _____ than art. (interesting)

다음 단어를 활용하여 비교급 또는 최상급 문장을 완성하세요.

1   The North Pole is _____ than Korea. (cold)

2   The hamster is _____ than the rabbit. (small)

3   Seoul is _____ than Busan. (big)

4   She is _____ than her sister. (beautiful)

5   The _____ subject for me is math. (difficult.)

6   Mt. Everest is _____ than Mt. Halla. (high)

7   Jeju island is the _____ island in Korea. (large)

8   The Nile is _____ than the Han River. (long)

9   My bag is _____ than his bag. (cheap)

10 Ann's book is _____ than yours. (thick)

11 The steel is _____ than the stone. (hard)

12 My father is the _____ man in our family. (old)

13 Her car is _____ than his. (expensive)

14 She is the _____ girl of my friends. (tall)

15 I have _____ money than you. (little)

16 Here is the _____ place in this town. (dangerous)

the North pole
북극

subject 과목

island 섬

thick 두꺼운

steel 강철

hard 단단한

place 장소

다음 우리말과 같도록 빈칸에 알맞은 말을 쓰세요.

1 The boy runs _____ the girl. (fast)

그 소년은 그 소녀보다 더 빨리 달린다.

2 Mr. Brown is _____ an actor. (popular)

Brown 씨는 배우만큼 인기가 많다.

3 She is _____ than a flower. (beautiful)

그녀는 꽃보다 더 아름답다.

4 Mt. Baekdu is _____ mountain in Korea. (high)

백두산은 한국에서 가장 높은 산이다.

5 My mom is _____ my dad. (young)

나의 엄마는 아빠보다 더 어리다.

6 This book is _____ the movie. (boring)

이 책은 그 영화보다 더 지루하다.

7 My brother is _____ Mark. (smart)

나의 남동생은 Mark만큼 영리하다.

8 Picasso is _____ artist in the world. (famous)

피카소는 세계에서 가장 유명한 화가이다.

9 The apple is _____ this orange. (sweet)

그 사과는 이 오렌지만큼 달지 않다.

10 We sell _____ cookies in Seoul. (good)

우리는 서울에서 가장 좋은 쿠키를 판다.

---

mountain 산
boring 지루한
artist 화가
world 세계, 세상
sweet 달콤한

다음 우리말과 같도록 빈칸에 알맞은 말을 쓰세요.

1 He is _____ boy in this town. (brave)

그는 이 마을에서 가장 용감한 소년이다.

2 You are _____ father in the world. (good)

당신은 세상에서 가장 훌륭한 아버지이다.

3 Today is _____ yesterday. (cold)

오늘은 어제보다 더 춥다.

4 Grandfather is _____ in my family. (old)

할아버지는 우리 가족 중에서 가장 나이가 많으시다.

5 Thomas is _____ a cat. (quick)

Thomas는 고양이만큼 빠르다.

6 She is _____ of the five. (busy)

그녀는 그 다섯 중에서 가장 바쁘다.

7 My dog is _____ your dog. (fat)

나의 개는 너의 개보다 더 뚱뚱하다.

8 Math is _____ science. (difficult)

수학은 과학만큼 어렵다.

9 This is _____ house in this city. (big)

이것은 이 도시에서 가장 큰 집이다.

10 _____ thing is the war. (bad)

가장 나쁜 것은 전쟁이다.

today 오늘
yesterday 어제
quick 빠른
thing 물건, 것

다음 주어진 문장을 참고하여 문장을 완성하세요.

weigh 무게가 나가다
rain 비가 오다

1 John is 140cm tall. Brian is 145cm tall.

→ Brian is _____ John.

2 The apple is one dollar. The orange is two dollars.

→ The orange is _____ the apple.

3 This ruler is 10cm long. That ruler is 10cm long, too.

→ This ruler is as _____.

4 The milk is one dollar. The Juice is two dollars.
The coke is three dollars.

→ The milk is _____ the three.

5 Joe is twelve years old. Dan is thirteen years old.

→ Joe is not _____ Dan.

6 Tony is 120cm tall. Nancy is 130cm tall.

→ Tony is not as _____.

7 Judy is five years old. Ann and Bob are six years old.

→ Judy is _____ the three.

8 The cat weighs 5kg. The dog weighs 5kg, too.

→ That cat is _____ heavy _____.

9 My brother gets up at 5 o'clock. I get up at 7 o'clock.

→ My brother gets up _____ I.

10 It rained 15ml in Seoul. It rained 30ml in Busan.

→ It rained in Busan _____ in Seoul.

다음 빈칸에 알맞은 말을 쓰세요.

I 대부분의 형용사나 부사는 원급에 **-er**을 붙여 _____을, **-est**를 붙여 _____을 만든다.

	비교급(최상급)	원급	비교급	최상급
대부분의 형용사, 부사	+-er(-est)	_____ fast	taller _____	_____ fastest
-e로 끝나는 형용사, 부사	+-r(-st)	large _____	_____ cuter	largest _____
모음1개+자음1개로 끝나는 형용사, 부사	마지막 자음 +-er(-est)	_____ fat	hotter _____	hottest _____
-y로 끝나는 형용사, 부사	y를 i로 바꾸고, -er(-est)	_____ easy	_____	happiest
3음절 이상 형용사, 부사	more(most) +형용사, 부사	beautiful popular	_____ _____ more popular	most beautiful _____ _____

〈불규칙 변화〉

원급	비교급	최상급
good, well bad, ill many, much little	_____ worse _____ _____	_____ _____ most _____

2 원급, 비교급, 최상급을 이용한 비교

① **as 원급 as**: ~만큼 ~하다

주어+동사	as ____ as	비교 대상

② **비교급+than**: ~보다 더 ~한

주어+동사	____ than	비교 대상

다음 문장에서 밑줄 친 부분을 바르게 고쳐 쓰세요.

dark 어두운
wood 목재

1 Your car is <u>largger</u> than mine. → _____

2 This place is as <u>darker</u> as that place. → _____

3 The steel is <u>hard</u> than the wood. → _____

4 This problem is the <u>easier</u> of the three. → _____

5 She is the <u>strong</u> people in the world. → _____

6 Her clothes are <u>nice</u> than his. → _____

7 You speak English <u>good</u> than I do. → _____

8 Tom is the <u>smarter</u> boy in this city. → _____

9 Today is as <u>hotter</u> as yesterday. → _____

10 Your bag is <u>newest</u> than hers. → _____

11 Mom gets up <u>early</u> than dad. → _____

12 Swimming is as <u>best</u> as running. → _____

13 She is the <u>more pretty</u> girl in the city. → _____

14 He is the tallest boy <u>of</u> my town. → _____

15 That girl is <u>fat</u> than this boy. → _____

16 The pants are <u>expensive</u> than the skirt. → _____

다음 주어진 문장과 같은 의미가 되도록 문장을 완성하세요.

cook 요리하다
husband 남편
important 중요한
be spoken 말해지다
animation 만화영화

1 This bag is heavier than that bag.

= That bag is _____ _____ this bag.

2 The chair is not as new as the table.

= The table is _____ _____ the chair.

3 He cooks better than his wife.

= She doesn't cook _____ _____ _____ her husband.

4 Peter doesn't run as fast as Brian.

= Brian _____ _____ than Peter.

5 Jeju is warmer than Seoul in December.

= Seoul is _____ _____ Jeju in December.

6 This is more important than any other work.

= This is _____ _____ _____ work.

7 Mt. Halla is not as high as Mt. Everest.

= Mt. Everest is _____ _____ Mt. Halla.

8 Seoul is larger than any other city in Korea.

= Seoul is _____ _____ _____ in Korea.

9 English is spoken more than Japanese.

= Japanese is spoken _____ _____ English.

10 The animation is not as interesting as the book.

= The book is _____ _____ _____ the animation.

다음 우리말과 같도록 주어진 말을 사용하여 영어로 쓰세요.

baseball 야구
live 살다
hair 머리카락
cheap 싼

1 수학은 가장 어려운 과목이다. (difficult, subject)

→ Math is _____

2 그 학생들은 야구보다 축구를 더 잘한다. (well, play)

→ The students _____

3 이 방은 저 방만큼 넓다. (large, room)

→ This room _____

4 Matt는 그의 반에서 가장 키가 큰 학생이다. (tall, class)

→ Matt is the _____

5 여자들이 남자들보다 더 오래 산다. (long, live)

→ Women _____

6 Sue의 머리카락은 Ann의 머리카락보다 더 짧다. (short, hair)

→ Sue's hair _____

7 이 사과는 그 넷 중에서 가장 크다. (big, four)

→ This apple _____

8 나의 어머니는 나의 아버지만큼 나이가 드셨다. (old, father)

→ My mother _____

9 이 차는 저 차보다 더 싸다. (cheap, car)

→ _____

10 이 산은 세상에서 가장 높다. (high, mountain)

→ _____

[1~3] 다음 중 비교급과 최상급이 <u>잘못된</u> 것을 고르세요.

1
① long – longer – longest
② well – better – best
③ nice – nicer – nicest
④ hot – hoter – hotest

2
① little – less – last
② large – larger – largest
③ thin – thinner – thinnest
④ famous – more famous – most famous

3
① bad – worse – worst
② pretty – more pretty – most pretty
③ lovely – lovelier – loveliest
④ many – more – most

[4~6] 다음 중 빈칸에 알맞은 말을 고르세요.

4 Her house is _____ than yours.
① expensive
② expensiver
③ more expensive
④ most expensive

5 You are the _____ mother in the world.
① more   ② less
③ most   ④ best

6 The apple is not as _____ as this orange.
① sweeter   ② sweetest
③ sweet   ④ more sweet

7 다음 중 빈칸에 들어갈 말이 나머지와 <u>다른</u> 것을 고르세요.
① Seoul is bigger _____ Busan.
② Tony is the tallest _____ in our class.
③ I get up earlier _____ Mike.
④ Science is easier _____ math for me.

8 다음 중 그림과 내용이 일치하는 것을 고르세요.

① A is faster than B.
② B is faster than C.
③ C is slower than A.
④ A is the slowest student.

9 다음 중 빈칸에 들어갈 말이 알맞게 짝지어진 것을 고르세요.

> Your book is _____ than mine.
> This book is the _____ one in this store.

① bigger – biggest   ② bigger – big
③ biggest – bigger   ④ big – bigger

[10~12] 다음 두 문장의 의미가 같도록 빈칸에 알맞은 말을 쓰세요.

10 This bag is heavier than that bag.
= That bag is _____ than this bag.

11 Mt. Halla is not as high as Mt. Baekdu.
= Mt. Baekdu is _____ _____ Mt. Halla.

12 The desk is newer than the sofa.
= The sofa is _____ _____ new _____ the desk.

13 다음 표를 보고, 빈칸에 알맞은 말을 쓰세요.

	Alex	Mark
Height	160cm	158cm

→ Alex is _____ _____ Mark. (tall)

[14~16] 다음 중 알맞은 문장을 고르세요.

14 ① Peter is smart than Jenny.
② She is more popular than her sister.
③ Jane's hair is longest than Julie's.
④ I am the happier woman in this town.

15 ① He is the strongest man in the world.
② A subway is more faster than a bus.
③ This is more cheap than that.
④ This is taller building in this city.

16 ① He is more shorter than Alice.
② This is as sweeter as that.
③ January is the coldest month.
④ Sue is the most thin girl in my class.

[17~18] 다음 밑줄 친 부분을 바르게 고쳐 쓰세요.

17 I play soccer as <u>good</u> as the other players.

→ _____

18 This apple is the biggest <u>in</u> the four.

→ _____

[19~20] 다음 주어진 문장을 참고하여 문장을 완성하세요.

19 Ashley is 140cm tall. Julie is 150cm tall.
→ Ashley is not as _____.

20 The eraser is one dollar. The ruler is two dollars.
→ The ruler is _____ than the eraser.

A 다음 표의 빈칸에 알맞은 말을 쓰세요.

	원급	비교급	최상급
1	ill	_____	_____
2	_____	warmer	_____
3	many	_____	_____
4	_____	_____	most famous

B 다음 그림과 일치하도록 괄호 안의 단어를 알맞게 쓰세요.

Joe(13살, 50kg)   Billy(11살, 40kg)

1 Joe is _____ than Billy. (old)

2 Joe is _____ than Billy. (heavy)

3 Billy's hair is _____ than Joe's. (long)

4 Billy is _____ than Joe. (short)

C 다음 표를 보고, 빈칸에 알맞은 말을 쓰세요.

	Chris	Amy	Mike	Sally
height(cm)	153	150	169	169
age(years old)	12	13	14	15

1 Sally is _____ tall _____ Mike. Sally는 Mike만큼 키가 크다.

2 Mike is _____ and _____ than Chris. Mike는 Chris보다 키도 크고 나이도 많다.

3 Amy is the _____ student of all. Amy는 모두 중에서 제일 작다.

Unit
4

조동사

조동사의 역할과 종류 및 특징을 이해할 수 있다.

조동사의 쓰임을 이해하고 활용할 수 있다.

동사 앞에서 동사의 뜻이 잘 전달되도록 도와주는 동사를 조동사라고 해요. 동사만으로는 '~할 수 있다', ~할 것이다'와 같은 말을 만들 수 없기 때문에 가능이나, 미래, 추측 등을 나타낼 때 조동사의 도움을 받아야 해요.

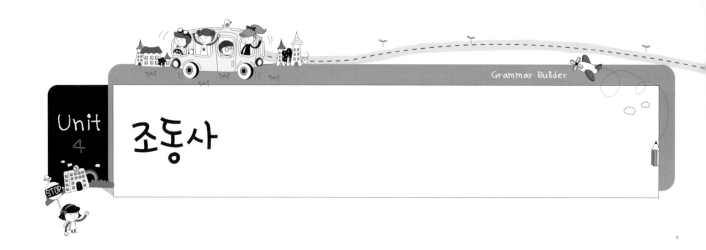

Unit
4

조동사

1. 조동사의 의미

동사 앞에서 동사의 의미를 분명하게 도와주는 동사를 조동사라고 한다.

He plays soccer. 그는 축구를 한다.

He can play soccer. 그는 축구를 할 수 있다. [가능]

He will play soccer. 그는 축구를 할 것이다. [미래]

He must play soccer. 그는 축구를 해야만 한다. [의무]

조동사	will	can	must	may
의미	(미래) ~할 것이다	(가능) ~할 수 있다 (허가) ~해도 된다	(의무) ~해도 된다 (추측) ~임에 틀림없다	(허락) ~해야 좋다 (추측) ~일지도 모른다
같은 표현	be going to	(가능) be able to	(의무) have to	–

▶ 조동사 will은 Unit 8 동사의 미래시제 **참고**

2. 조동사의 특징

조동사는 동사를 도와주는 동사이기 때문에 동사 없이 혼자 쓰일 수 없으며 반드시 동사와 같이 쓰이며, 조동사 뒤에는 항상 동사원형이 온다.

1. 조동사는 동사 앞에 온다.	She can dance. 그녀는 춤을 출 수 있다.
2. 조동사 뒤에는 항상 동사원형이 온다.	He will play soccer. plays (×) 그는 축구를 할 것이다.
3. 주어가 3인칭 단수라도 조동사에는 -(e)s를 붙이지 않는다.	She can play the piano. cans (×) 그녀는 피아노를 칠 수 있다.
4. 두 개의 조동사를 연속으로 사용할 수 없다.	He will can sing a song. (×) will이나 can 중 하나만 사용해야 한다.
5. 조동사의 부정문은 조동사 뒤에 not을 넣어 만든다.	She can dance. → She cannot dance. (부정문) 그녀는 춤을 출 수 없다.
6. 조동사의 의문문은 조동사를 문장 앞으로 보내고 문장 뒤에 물음표를 붙이면 된다.	She can dance. → Can she dance? (의문문) 그녀는 춤을 출 수 있니? – Yes, she can. (긍정) / No, she can't. (부정)

Pop Quiz   Ⅰ. 다음 괄호 안에서 알맞은 것을 고르세요.

❶ Tom (will, wills) go to school.   ❷ She can (ride, rides) a bike.

3. can - 능력, 가능

(1) can의 쓰임: ~할 수 있다(가능)

가능의 can은 be able to로 바꿔 쓸 수가 있는데, be able to 뒤에는 동사원형이 오며 be동사는 주어에 따라서 알맞은 be동사를 쓰면 된다.

[긍정문]   He can speak English well. 그는 영어를 잘 말할 수 있다.

   = He is able to speak English well.

[부정문]   He cannot[can't] speak English well. 그는 영어를 잘 말할 수 없다.

   = He is not[isn't] able to speak English well.

[의문문]　Can he speak English well? 그는 영어를 잘 말할 수 있니?

　　　　　= Is he able to speak English well?

can으로 물어보면 Yes나 No를 이용해 can으로 답을 하며(Yes, he can. (긍정) / No, he can't. (부정)), be able to로 물어보면 be동사의 의문문에 답하는 방식과 같다.

> Can I ~?는 '~해도 될까요?'라는 뜻으로 허가의 의미로도 사용된다.
> Can I open the door? 문을 좀 열어도 될까요?

(2) 조동사 will과 함께 쓰는 경우

2개의 조동사를 연속으로 사용할 수 없기 때문에, 이런 경우 can 대신 be able to를 사용하면 된다.

She will can pass the exam. (×) 그녀는 시험에 합격할 수 있을 것이다.

→ She will be able to pass the exam.

　　(조동사가 연속으로 사용된 경우)

4. must, may - 추측, 의무

(1) must: ~해야 한다(의무), ~임에 틀림없다(강한 추측)

must가 의무를 나타낼 때는 have to(3인칭일 경우에는 has to)로 바꿔 쓸 수 있다. 그러나 강한 추측으로 사용될 때는 have to로 바꿔 쓸 수 없다.

I must[=have to] go now. 나는 지금 가야 한다. (의무)

He must[≠has to] be tired. 그녀는 피곤한 것이 틀림없다. (강한 추측)

must의 부정문은 must not(금지)과 don't have to(불필요)를 사용해서 만든다.

(2) may: ~해도 좋다(허락), ~일지도 모른다(약한 추측)

May I use your phone? 너의 전화기를 사용해도 될까요? (허락)

She may be late. 그녀는 늦을지도 모른다. (약한 추측)

다음 빈칸에 들어갈 말을 〈보기〉에서 골라 번호를 쓰세요. (2개)

〈보기〉
① can ② am able to ③ is able to
④ are able to ⑤ must ⑥ have to ⑦ has to

rule 규칙
exercise 운동하다
Spanish 스페인어
understand 이해하다

1 He _____ ride a horse. (   )

그는 말을 탈 수 있다.

2 We _____ follow the rules. (   )

우리는 그 규칙을 따라야만 한다.

3 Peter _____ exercise every day. (   )

Peter는 매일 운동을 해야만 한다.

4 My sisters _____ speak Spanish. (   )

나의 누나들은 스페인어를 말할 수 있다.

5 I _____ understand this thick book. (   )

나는 이 두꺼운 책을 이해할 수 있다.

6 Tom and Dan _____ sing a song. (   )

Tom과 Dan은 노래를 불러야만 한다.

7 I _____ move this box alone. (   )

나는 이 상자를 홀로 옮길 수 있다.

8 Judy _____ take care of her sister. (   )

Judy는 그녀의 여동생을 돌 볼 수 있다.

9 She _____ take this bus. (   )

그녀는 이 버스를 타야만 한다.

10 He _____ play soccer on Sunday. (   )

그는 일요일에 축구를 할 수 있다.

다음 괄호 안에서 알맞은 것을 골라 동그라미 하세요.

1 Matt may (be, is) sick.

2 She (stay, stays) in her room.

3 Adam will (starts, start) soon.

4 My daughter can (rides, ride) a bike.

5 My sister and Amy must (goes, go) now.

6 John (meet, meets) Julia at the station.

7 I will (study, studies) math after school.

8 My uncle (speak, speaks) English well.

9 He may (go, goes) to the party tonight.

10 He must (do, does) the homework.

11 Tiffany (eat, eats) pizza for lunch.

12 I can (visit, visits) my grandparents.

13 My mom and dad may (be, are) late.

14 Her son (help, helps) them.

15 The little boy can (play, plays) the guitar.

16 She (clean, cleans) her room every day.

stay 머무르다
station 역
tonight 오늘밤
grandparent 조부모
guitar 기타
clean 청소하다

다음 괄호 안에서 알맞은 것을 골라 동그라미 하세요.

1 Jonathan can (passes, pass) the exam.

2 She has to (does, do) her homework.

3 She will (is, be) thirteen years old.

4 The police officer (rescue, rescues) the child.

5 You can (read, reads) a newspaper here.

6 Mary (have to, has to) win the game.

7 The cat may (eat, eats) that fish.

8 The girls are able to (draw, draws) pictures.

9 They (have to, has to) leave for London.

10 We (are, is) able to swim this weekend.

11 My brother may (bring, brings) my bag.

12 Ashley (chew, chews) the gum.

13 Billy must (turn, turns) off the radio.

14 He is able to (have, has) dinner there.

15 He will (be, is) able to finish the work.

16 It may (rain, rains) tomorrow.

exam 시험

rescue 구조하다

newspaper 신문

win 이기다

weekend 주말

chew 씹다

다음 주어진 말을 넣어 문장을 다시 쓰세요.

1 My sister leaves this town. (will)

→ _____

2 He buys the ticket. (may)

→ _____

3 The girl plays the piano in the hall. (can)

→ _____

4 The man swims in the lake. (be able to)

→ _____

5 She exercises for her health. (have to)

→ _____

6 Tom and Jane meet in the park. (be able to)

→ _____

7 Her brother makes model planes. (can)

→ _____

8 Alice goes to see a doctor. (must)

→ _____

9 My parents have lunch together. (will)

→ _____

10 My math textbook is in school. (must)

→ _____

ticket 표
hall 강당
health 건강
model 모형
textbook 교과서

다음 문장을 부정문으로 바꿔 다시 쓰세요.

drive 운전하다
garbage 쓰레기
Italian 이탈리아의
present 선물

1 My brother can fly the kite.

→ _____

2 He must write a letter to her. (금지)

→ _____

3 Sophia may come back home.

→ _____

4 Brian is able to drive a car.

→ _____

5 You must throw away garbage. (금지)

→ _____

6 Sarah may be late again.

→ _____

7 They must meet him in the gallery. (불필요)

→ _____

8 She can cook the Italian food.

→ _____

9 We are able to buy a present for him.

→ _____

10 Jack must wait for Peter. (불필요)

→ _____

다음 주어진 말을 활용하여 의문문으로 바꿔 다시 쓰세요.

obey 복종하다
castle 성
ask 묻다

1 Julie uses a computer. (can)

→ _____

2 My brother plays the guitar. (be able to)

→ _____

3 People obey the law. (must)

→ _____

4 I take a picture in the castle. (may)

→ _____

5 John and Tom go shopping with me. (be able to)

→ _____

6 I ask you a question. (may)

→ _____

7 She takes care of her brother. (must)

→ _____

8 Your father plays golf well. (be able to)

→ _____

9 You bring me the dictionary. (can)

→ _____

10 They bake a strawberry cake. (be able to)

→ _____

다음 문장을 지시대로 바꿔 쓰세요.

without ~ 없이
French 프랑스어
address 주소

1 You can borrow this book. (부정문)

→ _____

2 He can play computer games now. (의문문)

→ _____

3 She must wash the dishes. (부정문, 불필요)

→ _____

4 We are able to live without water. (부정문)

→ _____

5 They must finish the homework. (부정문, 금지)

→ _____

6 She can go home now. (의문문)

→ _____

7 Peter is able to speak French. (의문문)

→ _____

8 They may help the sick girl. (부정문)

→ _____

9 The kid is able to read and write. (부정문)

→ _____

10 The boy can remember his address. (의문문)

→ _____

다음 주어진 말을 활용하여 지시대로 바꿔 쓰세요.

key 열쇠

fix 고치다

1 They find the key in the room. (can, 부정문)

→ _____

2 Judy cleans her room now. (must, 긍정문)

→ _____

3 Mr. Smith helps the poor child. (긍정문, be able to)

→ _____

4 Ann comes back home by eight. (의문문, be able to)

→ _____

5 I draw your face there. (의문문, may)

→ _____

6 Tony fixes his bike. (의문문, be able to)

→ _____

7 He visits my house on Sunday. (must, 부정문, 불필요)

→ _____

8 Jonathan runs very fast. (must, 부정문, 금지)

→ _____

9 You go on a picnic on Friday. (can, 의문문)

→ _____

10 I will play soccer in the park. (be able to, 긍정문)

→ _____

Build Up 3

다음 문장을 지시대로 바꿔 고쳐 쓰세요.

plant 심다
flute 플루트
message 메시지
receive 받다

1 The boy can plant the flowers alone.

(부정문) _____

(의문문) _____

2 Tom is able to walk to the park.

(부정문) _____

(의문문) _____

3 You have a flute. Can you play the flute?

(대답, 긍정) _____

(대답, 부정) _____

4 You must leave my message.

(부정, 금지) _____

(부정, 불필요) _____

5 Is she able to receive the e-mail?

(대답, 긍정) _____

(대답, 부정) _____

6 We can play baseball at the playground.

(부정문) _____

(의문문) _____

7 They are able to buy the piano.

(부정문) _____

(의문문) _____

다음 빈칸에 알맞은 말을 쓰세요.

1 동사 앞에서 동사의 의미를 분명하게 도와주는 동사를 _____ 라고 한다.

조동사	will	can	must	may
의미	(미래) ~할 것이다	(가능) ~ _____ (허가) ~해도 된다	(의무) ~해야 한다 (추측) ~ _____	(허락) ~해도 좋다 (추측) ~ _____
같은 표현	be going to	be _____ (가능)	_____ (의무)	–

2 조동사의 특징

1. 조동사는 _____ 앞에 온다.	**He can play soccer.** 그는 축구를 할 수 있다.
2. 조동사 뒤에는 항상 동사의 _____이 온다.	**He will _____ soccer.** 그는 축구를 할 것이다.
3. 주어가 3인칭 단수라도 조동사에는 -(e)s를 붙이지 않는다.	**He can _____ the piano.** 그는 피아노를 칠 수 있다.
4. 두 개의 조동사를 연속으로 사용할 수 없다.	**He will can sing a song.** (×) **He will be _____ to sing a sing.** (O)
5. 조동사의 부정문은 조동사 뒤에 _____을 넣어 만든다.	**He can dance. → He cannot dance.** (부정문) 그는 춤을 출 수 없다.
6. 조동사의 의문문은 조동사를 문장 앞으로 보내고 문장 뒤에 물음표를 붙이면 된다.	**He can dance. → _____ he dance?** (의문문) 그는 춤을 출 수 있니? **– Yes, he can.** (긍정) / **_____, he can't.** (부정)

3 조동사의 문장 전환

(1) He _____ speak English. = He is able to speak English.

(2) Ashley must go now. = Ashley _____ _____ go now.

다음 문장에서 밑줄 친 부분을 고쳐 바르게 쓰세요.

1 We <u>cans</u> meet Matt in the library. → _____

2 She may <u>don't</u> come here. → _____

3 Judy <u>are</u> able to drive a car. → _____

4 You <u>has</u> to go home soon. → _____

5 May I <u>takes</u> a picture there? → _____

6 She and I <u>doesn't</u> have to hurry up. → _____

7 My brother must <u>is</u> sick. → _____

8 Tom will <u>can</u> go on a picnic. → _____

9 It may <u>rains</u> this weekend. → _____

10 She <u>musts</u> study math hard. → _____

11 We are able to <u>helps</u> our mother. → _____

12 They <u>cann't</u> cross the street. → _____

13 John <u>have</u> to move to New York. → _____

14 They <u>not must</u> answer the question. → _____

15 Mr. White is able to <u>making</u> a kite. → _____

16 Can you <u>goes</u> to the market with me? → _____

soon 곧
hurry 서두르다
cross 건너다
market 시장

조동사 • **87**

 Jump Up 3

다음 문장에서 틀린 부분을 바르게 고쳐 다시 문장을 쓰세요.

chopstick 젓가락
repeat 반복하다
history 역사
brush 닦다

1 James cans use the chopsticks.

→ _____

2 She have to repeat the word.

→ _____

3 Are you able to helping the sick people?

→ _____

4 John will can teach history.

→ _____

5 Peter and Mark must are very hungry.

→ _____

6 Her brother cann't fix the chair.

→ _____

7 He don't have to brush his teeth.

→ _____

8 You is able to finish your homework.

→ _____

9 It mays rain this afternoon.

→ _____

10 The kid is able not to draw a nice picture.

→ _____

다음 우리말과 같도록 주어진 말을 사용하여 영어로 쓰세요.

hunt 사냥하다
pass 합격하다
speak 말하다
practice 연습하다

1 그 왕은 그 큰 곰을 사냥해야만 한다. (hunt)
→ The king _____ the big bear.

2 오늘은 일요일이다. 나는 학교에 갈 필요가 없다. (go)
→ Today is Sunday. I _____ to school.

3 그는 열이 있다. 그는 아플지도 모른다. (sick)
→ He has a fever. He _____.

4 Jenny는 시험에 합격할 수 있다. (pass)
→ Jenny _____ the exam.

5 너는 이 컴퓨터를 사용할 수 없다. (use)
→ You _____ this computer.

6 그녀는 여기 일찍 도착하지 않을지도 모른다. (get)
→ She _____ here early.

7 우리는 그 경기에서 이길 수 있을까? (win)
→ Are we _____ the game?

8 너는 여기서 크게 말해서는 안 된다. (speak)
→ You _____ out loudly here.

9 그들은 새 우산들을 살 수 없다. (buy)
→ They aren't _____ new umbrellas.

10 피곤해 보인다. 축구를 연습할 필요가 없다. (practice)
→ You look tired. You _____ soccer.

[1~2] 다음 두 문장이 같은 뜻이 되도록 빈칸에 알맞은 말을 고르세요.

1

> Peter can fix the computer.
> = Peter _____ able to fix the computer.

① is   ② are
③ do   ④ does

2

> We must follow the rules.
> = We _____ to follow the rules.

① able   ② has
③ have   ④ may

3 다음 빈칸에 알맞은 것을 고르세요.

> My father is busy.
> He _____ come home early.

① can   ② may
③ may not   ④ don't have to

[4~6] 다음 우리말과 같도록 〈보기〉에서 알맞은 것을 골라 쓰세요.

> 〈보기〉 may can will must

4 너는 올해 영어 공부를 열심히 해야 한다.
→ You _____ study English hard this year.

5 저 작은 소년은 이 책을 읽을 수 있다.
→ That little boy _____ read this book.

6 그녀는 프랑스에 있는 삼촌을 방문할지도 모른다.
→ She _____ visit her uncle in France.

7 다음 빈칸에 공통으로 들어갈 말을 쓰세요.

> · Judy is able _____ drive a car.
> · I have _____ go to the park now.

→ _____

8 다음 중 우리말과 같도록 빈칸에 알맞은 것을 고르세요.

> 그들은 그것을 이해할 수 없다.
> = They _____ understand it.

① not able are to
② are not able to
③ able are not to
④ not are able to

[9~10] 다음 중 어법상 올바른 것을 고르세요.

9 ① It may rains this afternoon.
② They musts be tired now.
③ I will can ride a bike.
④ Lisa has to wait for her.

10 ① I can be able to go to the zoo.

② I can't play the piano well.

③ He cannot plays tennis well.

④ We not may go to the theater.

11 다음 두 문장의 의미가 같도록 빈칸에 알맞은 말을 쓰세요.

She must obey the parents.

= She _____ obey the parents.

12 다음 주어진 단어를 사용하여 문장을 완성하세요.

> 우리는 저것을 할 필요가 없다.
> (don't, to, do, have)

→ We _____ that.

13 다음 중 밑줄 친 must의 쓰임이 다른 것을 고르세요.

① They must take this bus.

② You must read all the books.

③ She must be sleepy now.

④ He must wear a suit at work.

14 다음 대화의 밑줄 친 부분 중 잘못된 것을 고르세요.

A: You ① must not ② are late for school tomorrow.

B: I know. ③ Can you call me tomorrow morning?

A: Sure, ④ I can.

15 다음 우리말을 영어로 가장 잘 옮긴 것을 고르세요.

> · 지금 내 말 들리니?

① Can you hear me now?

② Must you hear me now?

③ Will you hear me now?

④ May I hear you now?

16 다음 중 어법상 어색한 문장을 고르세요.

① You must be thirsty.

② He has to feed the cows.

③ She will can make many friends.

④ Can I close the window?

[17~18] 다음 밑줄 친 부분을 바르게 고쳐 쓰세요.

17 She don't have to do the work.

→ _____

18 We are not able to taking a picture here.

→ _____

[19~20] 다음 빈칸에 알맞은 조동사를 쓰세요.

19 You _____ clean the floor.

~해야만 한다

20 You _____ clean the black

~할 필요가 없다

board.

A 다음 두 문장이 같은 뜻이 되도록 빈칸에 알맞은 말을 쓰세요.

1 Mark and Peter can play baseball well.

= Mark and Peter ＿＿＿＿ ＿＿＿＿ ＿＿＿＿ play baseball well.

2 Sarah must see a doctor this afternoon.

= Sarah ＿＿＿＿ ＿＿＿＿ ＿＿＿＿ a doctor this afternoon.

B 다음 그림을 보고, must나 must not을 이용하여 문장을 완성하세요.

(×) (×) (×)

1 You ＿＿＿＿＿＿ snacks. (eat)

2 You ＿＿＿＿＿＿ quiet. (are)

3 You ＿＿＿＿＿＿ it. (touch)

C 다음 표를 보고, can이나 can't를 이용하여 문장을 완성하세요.

	play the piano	play the violin	play the cello
Chris	○	○	○
Mike	○	×	×
Billy	×	×	○

1 Chris and Mike ＿＿＿＿＿＿ play the ＿＿＿＿＿＿.

2 Mike and Billy ＿＿＿＿＿＿ play the ＿＿＿＿＿＿.

Unit 5

동사의 과거시제

be동사의 과거시제의 의미와 쓰임을 이해할 수 있다.

일반동사의 과거시제의 의미와 쓰임을 이해할 수 있다.

과거형 동사의 형태를 알고 문장에 활용할 수 있다.

지금 일어나고 있는 일을 현재라고 하고 앞으로 일어날 일을 미래하고 하며 지나간 일을

과거라고 해요. 영어에서는 지나간 과거의 일을 나타내기 위해서는 과거형 동사를 사용

하여 과거 문장을 나타내요. 과거형 문장은 보통 과거의 시간을 나타내는 수식어와

함께 써요.

Unit 5

동사의 과거시제

1. 동사의 과거시제

지금 일어나고 있는 일을 현재라고 하고 앞으로 일어날 일을 미래라고 하며 지나간 일을 과거라고 한다. 영어에서는 지나간 과거의 일을 나타내기 위해서는 과거형 동사를 사용하여 과거 문장을 나타낸다.

과거   현재   미래

〈과거〉

It was sunny yesterday.
어제는 맑았다.

I visited the museum.
나는 박물관을 방문했다.

〈현재〉

It is rainy today.
오늘은 비가 온다.

I study math at home.
나는 집에서 수학을 공부한다.

과거형 문장은 보통 과거 시간을 나타내는 수식어와 함께 쓰인다. yesterday(어제), the day before yesterday(그제), then(그때), last week(지난 주), last month(지난 달), a few days ago(며칠 전에), before(전에) 등

2. be동사의 과거형

be동사의 과거형 문장은 be동사의 과거형을 사용하여 나타내는데, be동사의 과거형은 was, were 두 가지이다. am과 is의 과거형은 was이고 are의 과거형은 were이다.

was, were	+명사, 형용사	~이었다, ~하였다
	+장소를 나타내는 말	~이 있었다

Mike was ten years old last year. Mike는 작년에 10살이었다.

It was windy yesterday. 어제는 바람이 불었다.

The boys were in the classroom. 그 소년들은 교실에 있었다.

Pop Quiz

1. 다음 be동사의 과거형을 골라 보세요.

❶ am (was, were) ❷ is (was, were) ❸ are (was, were)

3. 일반동사의 과거형

일반동사의 과거형은 동사에 -ed를 붙여서 만드는데, 이처럼 규칙적으로 변하는 동사가 있는가 하면 불규칙적으로 변하는 동사도 있다.

과거형 동사는
인칭이나 수의 영향을 받지 않는다.

(1) 규칙 변화: 동사원형+ed

만드는 방법		예
대부분의 동사	+-ed	walk–walked, play–played
e로 끝나는 동사	+-d	like–liked, dance–danced
자음+y로 끝나는 동사	y를 i로 고치고+-ed	cry–cried, carry–carried
단모음+단자음으로 끝나는 동사	마지막 자음을 하나 더 붙이고+-ed	stop–stopped, plan–planned
단모음+단자음으로 끝나지만 앞 음절에 강세가 있는 동사	+-ed	listen–listened, open–opened

He played the violin yesterday. 그는 어제 바이올린을 연주했다.

They helped the sick girl. 그들은 그 아픈 소녀를 도왔다.

(2) 불규칙 변화: 특별한 규칙이 없으므로 변화형을 외워둬야만 한다.

현재 – 과거	현재 –과거
cut(자르다) – cut(잘랐다)	think(생각하다) – thought(생각했다)
read(읽다) – read(읽었다)	go(가다) – went(갔다)
come(오다) – came(왔다)	see(보다) – saw(보았다)
run(달리다) – ran(달렸다)	eat(먹다) – ate(먹었다)
say(말하다) – said(말했다)	know(알다) – knew(알았다)
meet(만나다) – met(만났다)	give(주다) – gave(주었다)
do(하다) – did(했다)	buy(사다) – bought(샀다)

I saw my friends. 나는 나의 친구들을 보았다.

We bought the present for her. 우리는 그녀를 위해 선물을 샀다.

They read many books last month. 그들은 지난 달에 많은 책을 읽었다.

Pop Quiz **2.** 다음 동사의 과거형을 골라 보세요.

❶ cry (cried, cryed) ❷ run (runed, ran) ❸ do (did, doed)

〈불규칙 동사 변화표〉 불규칙 변화는 특별한 규칙이 없으므로 꼭 암기해 두자!

현재	과거	현재	과거
am, is/are ~ 이다	was/were ~ 이었다	fight 싸우다	fought 싸웠다
become 되다	became 되었다	find 발견하다	found 발견했다
begin 시작하다	began 시작했다	fly 날다	flew 날았다
bite 물다	bit 물었다	forget 잊다	forgot 잊었다
break 깨다	broke 깼다	forgive 용서하다	forgave 용서했다
bring 가져오다	brought 가져왔다	freeze 얼다	froze 얼었다
build 짓다	built 지었다	get 얻다	got 얻었다
burn 타다	burned/burnt 탔다	give 주다	gave 주었다
buy 사다	bought 샀다	go 가다	went 갔다
catch 잡다	caught 잡았다	grow 자라다	grew 자랐다
choose 선택하다	chose 선택했다	hang 걸다	hung 걸었다
cost 가격이 들다	cost 가격이 들었다	have 가지다, 먹다	had 가졌다, 먹었다
come 오다	came 왔다	hear 듣다	heard 들었다
cut 자르다	cut 잘랐다	hide 숨다	hid 숨었다
do 하다	did 했다	hit 치다	hit 쳤다
draw 그리다	drew 그렸다	hold 잡다	held 잡았다
drink 마시다	drank 마셨다	hurt 다치게 하다	hurt 다치게 했다
drive 운전하다	drove 운전했다	keep 유지하다	kept 유지했다
eat 먹다	ate 먹었다	leave 떠나다	left 떠났다
fall 떨어지다	fell 떨어졌다	lay 놓다	laid 놓았다
know 알다	knew 알았다	lie 거짓말을 하다	lied 거짓말을 했다
feed 먹이를 주다	fed 먹이를 줬다	lend 빌려주다	lent 빌려주었다
feel 느끼다	felt 느꼈다	let ~ 하게 하다	let ~ 하게 했다

현재	과거	현재	과거
lie 눕다	lay 누웠다	sing 노래를 하다	sang 노래를 했다
lose 지다	lost 졌다	sit 앉다	sat 앉았다
make 만들다	made 만들었다	sleep 자다	slept 잤다
mean 의미하다	meant 의미했다	speak 말하다	spoke 말했다
meet 만나다	met 만났다	spend 쓰다	spent 썼다
pay 지불을 하다	paid 지불을 했다	stand 서 있다	stood 서 있었다
put 두다, 놓다	put 뒀다, 놓았다	steal 훔치다	stole 훔쳤다
quit 그만두다	quit 그만두었다	swim 수영하다	swam 수영했다
read 읽다	read 읽었다	take 잡다	took 잡았다
ride 타다	rode 탔다	teach 가르치다	taught 가르쳤다
ring 울리다	rang 울렸다	tear 찢다	tore 찢었다
rise 일어나다	rose 일어났다	tell 말하다	told 말했다
run 달리다	ran 달렸다	think 생각하다	thought 생각했다
say 말하다	said 말했다	throw 던지다	threw 던졌다
see 보다	saw 보았다	understand 이해하다	understood 이해했다
sell 팔다	sold 팔았다	wake 깨우다	woke 깨웠다
send 보내다	sent 보냈다	wear 입다	wore 입었다
set 놓다, 두다	set 놓았다, 뒀다	win 이기다	won 이겼다
shut 닫다	shut 닫았다	write 쓰다	wrote 썼다

다음 동사의 과거형을 골라서 동그라미 하세요.

1 walk (walkked, walked)

2 hit (hitted, hit)

3 smile (smiled, smileed)

4 cut (cutted, cut)

5 stop (stoped, stopped)

6 bring (brought, bringed)

7 carry (carryed, carried)

8 have (had, haved)

9 look (looked, looks)

10 read (read, readed)

11 play (plaied, played)

12 go (goed, went)

13 dance (danced, danceed)

14 come (came, comed)

15 plan (planed, planned)

16 see (seed, saw)

17 like (liked, like)

18 are (were, was)

19 stay (staied, stayed)

20 is (were, was)

21 drop (dropped, droped)

22 think (thought, thinked)

23 work (works, worked)

24 give (gived, gave)

25 open (openned, opened)

26 buy (buyed, bought)

27 listen (listened, listenned)

28 know (knew, knowed)

29 visit (visited, visitted)

30 eat (eated, ate)

Check Up 2

다음 빈칸에 동사의 과거형을 쓰세요.

1 work _____

2 open _____

3 smile _____

4 stay _____

5 listen _____

6 wash _____

7 enjoy _____

8 plan _____

9 visit _____

10 drop _____

11 play _____

12 walk _____

13 turn _____

14 try _____

15 rain _____

16 love _____

17 marry _____

18 stop _____

19 show _____

20 pass _____

21 push _____

22 like _____

23 carry _____

24 worry _____

25 study _____

26 pull _____

27 cry _____

28 dance _____

29 look _____

30 live _____

다음 빈칸에 동사의 과거형을 쓰세요.

현재		과거		현재		과거
1	am, is		2	feel		
3	let		4	understand		
5	cost		6	shut		
7	begin		8	fly		
9	bite		10	forget		
11	break		12	forgive		
13	mean		14	speak		
15	build		16	get		
17	pay		18	stand		
19	catch		20	go		
21	quit		22	swim		
23	come		24	hang		
25	ride		26	teach		
27	do		28	hear		
29	draw		30	hide		
31	run		32	think		
33	drive		34	hold		
35	eat		36	hurt		
37	sell		38	wake		
39	feed		40	know		

 **Check Up 4**

다음 빈칸에 동사의 과거형을 쓰세요.

	현재	과거		현재	과거
1	lend		2	set	
3	are		4	fight	
5	become		6	find	
7	write		8	sing	
9	lose		10	sit	
11	make		12	sleep	
13	bring		14	freeze	
15	meet		16	spend	
17	buy		18	give	
19	put		20	steal	
21	choose		22	grow	
23	read		24	take	
25	cut		26	have	
27	ring		28	win	
29	rise		30	tell	
31	drink		32	hit	
33	say		34	throw	
35	see		36	leave	
37	fall		38	keep	
39	send		40	wear	

다음 괄호 안에서 알맞은 동사를 골라 동그라미 하세요.

1 They (were, was) very happy.

2 Tom (were, was) late for the meeting.

3 I (went, goed) to a concert with my family.

4 The apples (was, were) fresh.

5 Her mother (make, made) a cake for her.

6 I (was, were) twelve years old last year.

7 She (looked, look) at the bears.

8 We (are, were) very busy yesterday.

9 My mother (gived, gave) the gift to me.

10 Mike and Jane (were, was) my close friends.

11 It (was, were) cold a few days ago.

12 Peter (ate, eated) an orange this morning.

13 He and she (was, were) in the library then.

14 I (stopped, stoped) in front of the bank.

15 The problems (was, were) difficult.

16 They (play, played) baseball yesterday.

meeting 회의
concert 콘서트
fresh 신선한
gift 선물
close 친한

다음 괄호 안에서 알맞은 동사를 골라 동그라미 하세요.

1 She (buys, buyed, bought) a wallet yesterday.

2 Dan (stays, staied, stayed) home last weekend.

3 The children (is, was, were) sad then.

4 I (study, studyed, studied) history last month.

5 They (fight, fighted, fought) each other yesterday.

6 She (read, readed, reads) books last week.

7 Joan (teached, teachs, taught) math six years ago.

8 They (make, made, makes) a big kite last spring.

9 I (draw, drew, drawed) sunflowers last night.

10 He (leaves, leaved, left) for Japan last Sunday.

11 Joseph (has, haved, had) a puppy last year.

12 It (is, was, were) hot the day before yesterday.

13 Tony (build, buled, built) the house last month.

14 You (meeted, meet, met) her a few minutes ago.

15 Jonathan (helps, helped, helpt) a man yesterday.

16 He (finds, finded, found) the treasure last fall.

wallet 지갑
fight 싸우다
sunflower 해바라기
build 짓다
treasure 보물

다음 밑줄 친 동사를 과거형으로 고쳐 다시 쓰세요.

subway 지하철
begin 시작하다
broken 부서진
cold 감기
gate 대문
voice 목소리

1 Sam and John <u>are</u> kind police officers.

→ _____

2 The young girl <u>is</u> very pretty.

→ _____

3 Molly <u>goes</u> to the subway with him.

→ _____

4 She <u>teaches</u> science at school.

→ _____

5 Many students <u>clean</u> the street.

→ _____

6 The school <u>begins</u> at nine o'clock.

→ _____

7 My father <u>fixes</u> the broken bike.

→ _____

8 Julie <u>catches</u> a bad cold.

→ _____

9 They <u>stand</u> in front of the gate.

→ _____

10 Tony and Brian <u>hear</u> her voice.

→ _____

 **Build Up 2**

다음 괄호 안의 동사를 이용하여 과거형 문장을 만드세요.

postcard 엽서
free 자유로운
way 길
lose 잃어버리다
leave 떠나다

1 She _____ a postcard to her father. (write)

2 They _____ free last Saturday. (be)

3 The train _____ at ten a.m. yesterday. (start)

4 My mom _____ a skirt for my sister. (buy)

5 She _____ about him last night. (think)

6 I _____ the way to the hospital. (know)

7 Thomas _____ his uncle last week. (visit)

8 Ann _____ her homework then. (finish)

9 We _____ the concert with Jenny. (go)

10 He _____ to the station a few days ago. (run)

11 They _____ and danced last night. (sing)

12 I _____ Billy at the museum last month. (meet)

13 He _____ his watch last year. (lose)

14 Judy _____ back from London yesterday. (come)

15 Peter _____ here a few minutes ago. (be)

16 She _____ for Daejeon three hours ago. (leave)

다음 괄호 안의 동사를 알맞은 형태로 고쳐 쓰세요.

city hall 시청
move 움직이다
invent 발명하다
bottom 바닥
airport 공항
steal 훔치다

1 He _____ to the city hall yesterday. (drive)

2 The earth _____ around the sun. (move)

3 Mr. Smith _____ a lawyer last year. (become)

4 We _____ really happy then. (be)

5 One day _____ 24 hours, 1440 minutes. (be)

6 King Sejong _____ Hangeul in 1443. (invent)

7 Joe _____ camping with the friends last Friday. (go)

8 Water _____ from the top to the bottom. (flow)

9 She _____ at the airport four hours ago. (arrive)

10 The sun _____ in the east. (rise)

11 Susan _____ the picture in 1985. (draw)

12 Julie _____ the bike a few days ago. (ride)

13 We _____ the building there last month. (build)

14 A thief _____ money in my bag then. (steal)

15 I _____ some milk every morning. (drink)

16 The hunters _____ the deer last week. (catch)

다음 빈칸에 알맞은 말을 쓰세요.

1 지나간 일을 과거라고 하는데, 과거 문장은 _____ 동사를 써서 나타낸다. 또한 과거 문장은 과거 시간을 나타내는 수식어와 함께 쓰인다.

→ _____(어제), the day _____ yesterday(그제), then(그때), _____ week(지난 주), _____ month(지난 달), a few days _____(며칠 전에) 등

2 be동사 am과 is의 과거형은 _____이고 are의 과거형은 _____이다.

3 일반동사 과거형의 규칙변화는 보통 동사에 -ed를 붙여 만드는데,

만드는 방법		예
대부분의 동사	+-_____	walk-_____, play-_____
e로 끝나는 동사	+-_____	like-_____, dance-_____
자음+y로 끝나는 동사	y를 i로 고치고+-ed	cry-_____, carry-_____
단모음+단자음으로 끝나는 동사	마지막 _____을 하나 더 붙이고+-ed	stop-_____, plan-_____
단모음+단자음으로 끝나지만 앞 음절에 강세가 있는 동사	+-ed	listen-_____, open-_____

4 일반동사 과거형의 불규칙 변화는 특별한 규칙이 없다.

현재 - 과거		현재 - 과거	
cut	- _____	think	- _____
_____	- came	_____	- saw
say	- _____	_____	- knew
_____	- met	give	- _____

다음 문장에서 동사를 시제에 맞게 바르게 고쳐 쓰세요.

1 My mother is at the bookstore then. → _____

2 She loses the watch yesterday. → _____

3 I play the guitar there last night. → _____

4 He lives in the US two years ago. → _____

5 They take a walk three hours ago. → _____

6 She meets Mr. Brown last Sunday. → _____

7 Kate pays twenty dollars for it then. → _____

8 Eric passes the exam last month. → _____

9 She finds a wallet a few hours ago. → _____

10 Dan and I are in China last year. → _____

11 He reads the poem before. → _____

12 We stay at home last weekend. → _____

13 I see the movie a few days ago. → _____

14 You finish the work two hours ago. → _____

15 Alice becomes a teacher last year. → _____

16 Bill collects the many coins then. → _____

bookstore 서점
walk 산책
pay 지불하다
poem 시
coin 동전

다음 문장에서 동사 부분을 바르게 고쳐 문장을 다시 쓰세요.

wear 입다
floor 바닥
rope 밧줄
hurt 다치다
end 끝나다

1 Dorothy wears a hat last Sunday.

→ _____

2 He droped his pencil on the floor.

→ _____

3 We have fun last weekend.

→ _____

4 Adam writed the novel in 1996.

→ _____

5 John finded the ring under the bed then.

→ _____

6 Mark cutted the rope with a knife.

→ _____

7 Emily hurted her arm last Saturday.

→ _____

8 Sophie heared the news two hours ago.

→ _____

9 Sue telled me the story two weeks ago.

→ _____

10 The class endded at three p.m. yesterday.

→ _____

다음 우리말과 같도록 주어진 말을 사용하여 영어로 쓰세요.

beach 해변
magazine 잡지
promise 약속

1 그들은 지난 여름에 해변에 갔었다. (go, beach)

→ _____ last summer.

2 그저께는 바람이 불었다. (be, windy)

→ _____ the day before yesterday.

3 나는 어제 시장에서 음식을 샀다. (buy, food)

→ _____ at the market yesterday.

4 그녀는 그 당시 영어를 잘 했다. (speak, well)

→ _____ at that time.

5 우리는 며칠 전에 그 경기에서 이겼다. (win, game)

→ _____ a few days ago.

6 그는 지난 밤에 11시에 잠자리에 들었다. (go, bed)

→ _____ at eleven last night.

7 James는 그 잡지를 오후에 읽었다. (read, magazine)

→ _____ in the afternoon.

8 Joe는 어제 공원에서 그의 개를 잃어버렸다. (lose, dog)

→ _____ in the park yesterday.

9 나는 그때 그에게 메시지를 보냈다. (send, message)

→ _____ to him then.

10 Nick은 지난 주에 그 약속을 지켰다. (keep, promise)

→ _____ last week.

1 다음 중 동사의 원형과 과거형이 바르게 짝지어진 것을 고르세요.

① plan – planed
② dance – danced
③ listen – listenning
④ carry – carryed

[2~3] 다음 중 동사의 과거형이 <u>잘못</u> 연결된 것을 고르세요.

2　① cut – cut　　② read – read
　　③ hurt – hurt　　④ keep – keep

3　① begin – began ② come – came
　　③ swim – swom ④ write – wrote

4 다음 문장의 빈칸에 알맞지 <u>않은</u> 것을 고르세요.

> I _____ a few days ago.

① had fun
② went to a movie
③ sent an e-mail
④ wear a hat

[5~6] 다음 문장의 빈칸에 들어갈 말로 알맞은 것을 고르세요.

5 They _____ to Disneyland last month.
　　① go　　　　② goes
　　③ went　　　④ going

6 She met him at the station _____.
① now　　　　② yesterday
③ tomorrow　　④ next week

7 다음 괄호 안의 단어를 알맞은 형태로 고쳐 대화를 완성하세요.

> A: What did you do last summer vacation?
> B: I _____ swimming with my friends. (go)

→ _____

8 다음 문장을 과거형으로 바꿀 때 알맞은 것을 <u>고르세요.</u>

> They stand in front of the gate.

① They stands in front of the gate.
② They standed in front of the gate.
③ They stood in front of the gate.
④ They standing in front of the gate.

9 다음 우리말과 같도록 빈칸에 들어갈 알맞은 것을 고르세요.

> 나는 어제 7시에 저녁을 먹었다.
> = _____ at seven yesterday.

① I eat dinner
② I ate dinner
③ I eated dinner
④ I eats dinner

[10~11] 다음 문장에서 밑줄 친 부분을 바르게 고쳐 쓰세요.

10 Bill <u>think</u> about Amy last night.

→ _____

11 Sarah <u>is</u> here a few minutes ago.

→ _____

[12~13] 다음 우리말과 같도록 주어진 단어를 활용하여 문장을 완성하세요.

12 그는 지난 달에 그의 시계를 잃어버렸다. (lose, watch)

→ _____

13 나는 며칠 전에 영화를 보았다. (see, movie)

→ _____

[14~16] 다음 중 바르지 않은 문장을 고르세요.

14 ① The birds flew away.
② He wore a funny hat and shoes.
③ She and he was in London.
④ You often hid under the table.

15 ① She asked a lot of questions.
② Your sister sang very well.
③ I cook pasta last weekend.
④ The student opened the door.

16 ① It rained a lot last year.
② He has a good time then.
③ My father read a newspaper.
④ She climbed the mountain yesterday.

[17~18] 다음 그림을 보고, 주어진 문장을 완성하세요.

17

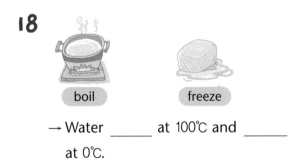

last year   this year

→ Harry _____ last year, but he _____ this year.

18

boil   freeze

→ Water _____ at 100℃ and _____ at 0℃.

[19~20] 다음 괄호 안의 동사를 알맞은 형태로 고쳐 쓰세요.

19 Mike _____ the story to Jane three days ago. (tell)

20 She _____ in Seoul five years ago. (live)

A 다음 글을 읽고, 동사를 과거형으로 바꾸어 다시 쓰세요.

Yesterday is a very exciting day for me. My classmates go on a trip to the fire station. We go to the fire station by bus, but it rains. We eat lunch inside the fire station with all the fire fighters. They are nice and funny. We get on the fire truck and ring the bell on the truck. And we walk around the fire station. I see a dog. The dog is a dalmatian. It is black and white. It is a great fun day!

B 다음 Amy에 관한 표를 보고, 빈칸에 알맞은 말을 쓰세요.

Two Years Ago	Now
have short hair	have long hair
go to the library every day	go to the library on Sundays

1 Amy _____ hair two years ago. She _____ hair now.

2 Two years ago, she _____ the library every day. She _____ the library on Sundays now.

과거시제의 부정문, 의문문

과거형 문장에서 부정문과 의문문의 의미와 쓰임을 이해할 수 있다.

과거형 문장에서 be동사의 부정문과 의문문을 만들 수 있다.

과거형 문장에서 일반동사의 부정문과 의문문을 만들 수 있다.

be동사 과거형의 부정문은 be동사 was나 were 뒤에 not을 붙여서 만들고 일반동사 과거형의 부정문은 일반동사 앞에 didn't를 붙여서 만들어요. be동사 과거형의 의문문은 be동사 was나 were를 주어 앞에 쓰고 문장 끝에 물음표를 붙이며 일반동사 과거형의 의문문은 Did를 주어 앞에 쓰고 문장 끝에 물음표를 붙여요.

Unit 6

과거시제의 부정문, 의문문

1. be동사 과거형의 부정문, 의문문

(1) 부정문

현재형 문장의 부정문은 be동사 am, are, is 다음에 not을 붙여서 만든다. 과거형 문장의 부정문은 현재형 문장과 마찬가지로 be동사 was, were 다음에 not을 붙여서 만든다.

주어	현재형 문장의 부정문	과거형 문장의 부정문
1인칭 단수(I)	am + not	was + not(= wasn't)
2인칭, 복수 (You, We, They, My books)	are + not(= aren't)	were + not(= weren't)
3인칭 단수(She, He, It, My book, Peter, Jane)	is + not(= isn't)	was + not(= wasn't)

〈be동사 과거형 문장의 부정문〉

She was not(= wasn't) hungry then.
그녀는 그때 배고프지 않았다.

They were not(= weren't) in the library.
그들은 도서관에 있지 않았다.

축약형:
was not = wasn't,
were not = weren't

(2) 의문문

현재형 문장의 의문문과 마찬가지로 과거형 문장의 의문문은 be동사인 was나 were를 주어 앞에 쓰고 문장 끝에 물음표를 붙인다.

현재형 문장의 의문문	과거형 문장의 의문문
Am+주어(1인칭 단수 주어) ~?	Was+주어(1인칭 단수 주어) ~?
Are+주어(2인칭, 복수 주어) ~?	Were+주어(2인칭 복수 주어) ~?
Is+주어(3인칭 단수 주어) ~?	Was+주어(3인칭 단수 주어) ~?

〈be동사 과거형 문장의 의문문과 대답〉

Was he in Seoul last year? 그는 작년에 서울에 있었니?

- Yes, he was. 응, 그랬어. (긍정)

- No, he wasn't. 아니, 그렇지 않았어. (부정)

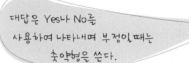

대답은 Yes나 No를 사용하여 나타내며 부정일 때는 축약형을 쓴다.

Pop Quiz　　Ⅰ. 다음 괄호 안에서 알맞은 것을 고르세요.

❶ I (was, were) not at home.　　❷ We (was, were) not sick.

2. 일반동사 과거형의 부정문과 의문문

(1) 부정문

현재형 문장의 부정문은 일반동사 앞에 don't나 doesn't를 붙여서 만든다. 과거형 문장의 부정문은 주어의 인칭에 관계없이 did not(=didn't)를 쓰고 동사원형을 쓰면 된다.

주어	현재형 문장의 부정문	과거형 문장의 부정문
1인칭 단수(I)	do not(=don't)+동사원형	did+not(=didn't) +동사원형
2인칭, 복수 (You, We, They, My books)	do not(=don't)+동사원형	did+not(=didn't) +동사원형
3인칭 단수(She, He, It, My book, Peter, Jane)	does+not(=doesn't)+동사원형	did+not(=didn't) +동사원형

〈일반동사 과거형 문장의 부정문〉

I did not(=didn't) know her name. 나는 그녀의 이름을 몰랐다.

He did not(=didn't) join the club. 그는 그 클럽에 가입하지 않았다.

(2) 의문문

현재형 의문문에서는 주어에 따라 문장 앞에 Do나 Does를 사용했지만 과거형에서는 do와 does의 과거형인 did를 사용하여 나타낸다.

현재형 문장의 의문문	과거형 문장의 의문문
Do+주어(1, 2인칭, 복수 주어)+동사원형 ~?	Did+주어+동사원형 ~?
Does+주어(3인칭 단수 주어)+동사원형~?	

〈일반동사 과거형 문장의 의문문과 대답〉

Did you meet Joan yesterday? 너는 어제 Joan을 만났니?

– Yes, I did. 응, 나는 그랬어. (긍정)

– No, I didn't. 아니, 나는 그렇지 않았어. (부정)

Did she meet Brian yesterday? 그녀는 어제 Brian을 만났니?

– Yes, she did. 응, 그녀는 그랬어. (긍정)

– No, she didn't. 아니, 그녀는 그렇지 않았어. (부정)

대답은 Yes나 No로 did를 사용하여 나타내며 부정일 때는 축약형을 쓴다.

┌─────────┐
│ Pop Quiz │ **2.** 다음 괄호 안에서 알맞은 것을 고르세요.
└─────────┘
❶ You (did, do) not like cats then.

❷ (Does, Did) he live here two years ago?

다음 문장을 지시대로 바꿀 때, 빈칸에 알맞은 말을 쓰세요.

luggage 짐
spend 소비하다
crosswalk 횡단보도
crop 농작물
help 도움

1 They carried the luggage into the room. (부정문)

→ They ＿＿＿＿ ＿＿＿＿ the luggage into the room.

2 She spent a lot of money then. (의문문)

→ ＿＿＿＿ she ＿＿＿＿ a lot of money?

3 The people were in the library. (부정문)

→ The people ＿＿＿＿ ＿＿＿＿ in the library.

4 Peter found his key under the bed. (부정문)

→ Peter ＿＿＿＿ ＿＿＿＿ his key under the bed.

5 Sally stopped in front of the crosswalk. (의문문)

→ ＿＿＿＿ Sally ＿＿＿＿ in front of the crosswalk?

6 My mother drove to the post office. (부정문)

→ My mother ＿＿＿＿ ＿＿＿＿ to the post office.

7 The farmer sold the crops at the market. (의문문)

→ ＿＿＿＿ the farmer ＿＿＿＿ the crops at the market?

8 Your ruler was on the TV yesterday. (부정문)

→ Your ruler ＿＿＿＿ ＿＿＿＿ on the TV yesterday.

9 Her sister needed his help. (의문문)

→ ＿＿＿＿ her sister ＿＿＿＿ his help?

10 They met Billy last weekend. (의문문)

→ ＿＿＿＿ they ＿＿＿＿ Billy last weekend?

다음 문장을 지시대로 바꿀 때, 빈칸에 알맞은 말을 쓰세요.

frog 개구리
dictionary 사전
lying 거짓말
cabin 오두막

1 He played soccer with his friends. (부정문)

→ He _____ _____ soccer with his friends.

2 Tom and Jack caught some frogs. (부정문)

→ Tom and Jack _____ _____ some frogs.

3 Brian saw a movie on Sunday. (의문문)

→ _____ Brian _____ a movie on Sunday?

4 His mother was hungry then. (의문문)

→ _____ his mother _____ then?

5 Judy gave a new dictionary to him. (부정문)

→ Judy _____ _____ a new dictionary to him.

6 People believed the boy's lying. (의문문)

→ _____ people _____ the boy's lying?

7 Mark and Sam were late again. (의문문)

→ _____ Mark and Sam _____ again?

8 He built the cabin with the carpenters. (부정문)

→ He _____ _____ the cabin with the carpenters.

9 Kate wrote a letter to her friend. (의문문)

→ _____ Kate _____ a letter to her friend?

10 The student understood the problem. (부정문)

→ The student _____ _____ the problem.

다음 주어진 문장을 부정문으로 바꿔 다시 쓰세요.

1 Amy and Alice were young then.

→ _____

2 The Jacket was expensive.

→ _____

3 He was interested in soccer.

→ _____

4 We were tired and thirsty.

→ _____

5 It was hot the day before yesterday.

→ _____

6 My father was a fire fighter.

→ _____

7 Susan was afraid of dogs.

→ _____

8 Your sneakers were very dirty.

→ _____

9 Jenny was in the classroom then.

→ _____

10 The tomatoes were in the bowl.

→ _____

expensive 비싼
interested 관심 있는
thirsty 목이 마른
fire fighter 소방관
afraid 두려워하는
sneaker 운동화
bowl 그릇, 사발

다음 주어진 문장을 부정문으로 바꿔 다시 쓰세요.

1 He made the bench a week ago.

→ _____

2 She ate two pieces of cake.

→ _____

3 She finished the work yesterday.

→ _____

4 Mark knew the way to the gallery.

→ _____

5 They bought vegetables then.

→ _____

6 She enjoyed the party last night.

→ _____

7 He had a nice car last year.

→ _____

8 Matt read a newspaper yesterday.

→ _____

9 We played the piano well.

→ _____

10 My family went fishing last week.

→ _____

gallery 미술관
vegetable 야채
fishing 낚시

다음 주어진 문장을 의문문으로 바꿔 다시 쓰세요.

call 전화하다
Canada 캐나다
theater 극장

1 She lived in New York two years ago.

→ _____

2 You were late for the meeting yesterday.

→ _____

3 The people had a nice winter vacation.

→ _____

4 The window was broken then.

→ _____

5 His brother called you last week.

→ _____

6 Nick left here three months ago.

→ _____

7 Susie planted the flowers in the garden.

→ _____

8 It was cold in Canada at that time.

→ _____

9 Tom and Ann saw a movie at the theater.

→ _____

10 Your mom and dad were in England.

→ _____

다음 질문에 Yes와 No로 시작하는 대답을 쓰세요.

education 교육
save 저축하다
blouse 블라우스
hole 구멍
sound 소리

1 Was Matt interested in the education?
→ Yes, _____ . / No, _____ .

2 Did you go to school last Sunday?
→ Yes, _____ . / No, _____ .

3 Were Dan and Joseph your friends?
→ Yes, _____ . / No, _____ .

4 Was Jane twelve years old last year?
→ Yes, _____ . / No, _____ .

5 Did they save money for her birthday?
→ Yes, _____ . / No, _____ .

6 Did Mrs. Smith wear a white blouse?
→ Yes, _____ . / No, _____ .

7 Did Bill and Tom find the big hole?
→ Yes, _____ . / No, _____ .

8 Did he run to the playground?
→ Yes, _____ . / No, _____ .

9 Were Paul and Jane at the zoo?
→ Yes, _____ . / No, _____ .

10 Did she hear the strange sound?
→ Yes, _____ . / No, _____ .

다음 주어진 문장을 지시대로 바꿔 다시 쓰세요.

break 깨뜨리다
kick 차다
diary 일기

1 Kevin talked with the friends. (부정문)

→ _____

2 He broke the window yesterday. (의문문)

→ _____

3 Thomas kicked the ball in the park. (부정문)

→ _____

4 My sister wrote the diary last night. (의문문)

→ _____

5 The student asked some questions. (의문문)

→ _____

6 They drank milk in the morning. (부정문)

→ _____

7 My father taught math at school. (부정문)

→ _____

8 The boy carried the heavy box. (의문문)

→ _____

9 She listened to music last night. (의문문)

→ _____

10 The girl swam with the mother. (부정문)

→ _____

다음 주어진 문장을 지시대로 바꿔 다시 쓰세요.

visitor 방문객
climb 오르다
spider 거미

1 Eric rode a horse two hours ago. (의문문)

→ _____

2 The visitor saw beautiful towers there. (의문문)

→ _____

3 The men climbed up the mountain. (부정문)

→ _____

4 The baby slept on the bed then. (의문문)

→ _____

5 It did not rain a few days ago. (긍정문)

→ _____

6 The spider came down the tree. (부정문)

→ _____

7 Sally had a great summer vacation. (의문문)

→ _____

8 They cleaned the classroom yesterday. (의문문)

→ _____

9 He received an e-mail from her. (부정문)

→ _____

10 My brother spoke Chinese well. (부정문)

→ _____

다음 주어진 문장을 지시대로 바꿔 다시 쓰세요.

1 Kate made the same mistake. (부정문)

→ _____

2 She put her ring here yesterday. (부정문)

→ _____

3 The kid remembered you at that time. (의문문)

→ _____

4 Huck painted the wall last month. (의문문)

→ _____

5 The drivers were busy and tired. (부정문)

→ _____

6 Ashley bought a new sweater. (부정문)

→ _____

7 Her cousin was young and pretty. (의문문)

→ _____

8 Joe passed the exam last week. (의문문)

→ _____

9 They were thirteen years old last year. (의문문)

→ _____

10 The judge punished the bad man. (부정문)

→ _____

mistake 실수
remember 기억하다
wall 벽
driver 운전사
judge 재판관
punish 벌을 주다

다음 빈칸에 알맞은 말을 쓰세요.

1 be동사 현재형 문장의 부정문은 be동사 _____, _____, _____ 다음에 not을 붙여서 만든다. 과거형 문장의 부정문은 be동사 was나 were 다음에 _____을 붙이며, was not의 축약형은 _____이고 were not의 축약형은 _____이다.

2 be동사 과거형 문장의 의문문은 be동사 was나 were를 문장 앞에 쓴다.

현재형 문장의 의문문	과거형 문장의 의문문
Am+주어(1인칭 단수 주어) ~?	_____+주어(1인칭 단수 주어) ~?
Are+주어(2인칭, 복수 주어) ~?	_____+주어(2인칭, 복수 주어) ~?
Is+주어(3인칭 단수 주어) ~?	_____+주어(3인칭 단수 주어) ~?

3 일반동사 과거형 문장의 부정문은 주어의 인칭에 관계없이 did not(= _____)를 쓰고 동사원형을 쓴다.

주어	현재형 문장의 부정문	과거형 문장의 부정문
1인칭 단수(I)		
2인칭, 복수(You, We, They, My books)	_____+not(=don't)	did+not(= _____)
3인칭 단수(She, He, It, My book, Peter, Jane)	_____+not(=doesn't)	

4 일반동사 과거형 문장의 의문문은 문장의 맨 앞에 _____를 쓴다. 이때 뒤에 오는 동사는 반드시 동사원형을 쓴다.

현재형 문장의 의문문	과거형 문장의 의문문
Do+주어(1, 2인칭, 복수 주어) ~?	_____+주어 ~?
_____+주어(3인칭 단수 주어) ~?	

다음 주어진 문장을 의문문으로 바꾸고 대답도 올바르게 완성하세요.

solve 풀다
riddle 수수께끼
pilot 조종사
cave 동굴

1 Tom was at the market.

→ _____ – No, _____.

2 Mark solved the riddle.

→ _____ – Yes, _____.

3 They were so happy then.

→ _____ – Yes, _____.

4 The man caught a bear.

→ _____ – No, _____.

5 She read the novel yesterday.

→ _____ – Yes, _____.

6 Her father was a pilot.

→ _____ – Yes, _____.

7 The bats lived in this cave.

→ _____ – No, _____.

8 It rained last Sunday.

→ _____ – Yes, _____.

9 The shoes were cheap.

→ _____ – No, _____.

10 They won the game last month.

→ _____ – Yes, _____.

다음 문장에서 틀린 부분에 ×표하고 바르게 고쳐 다시 쓰세요.

shelf 선반
popular 인기 있는
field 들판
smile 미소를 짓다
last 마지막의, 지난

1 Ann didn't made a big pizza then. → _____

2 Was Amy and Tony at the party? → _____

3 Did she looked at the flowers? → _____

4 I didn't got up at eight yesterday. → _____

5 Do the women buy hairpins then? → _____

6 Tom not put the book on the shelf. → _____

7 Did she sleeps well last night? → _____

8 My sister didn't called you yesterday. → _____

9 Jill lose the wallet a few days ago. → _____

10 They do not work hard last week. → _____

11 Were the food popular in the country? → _____

12 The weather didn't nice at that time. → _____

13 The farmers was not in the field. → _____

14 Jonathan did not smiles at me. → _____

15 Did he spent any money last Sunday? → _____

16 The last train didn't left at eleven p.m. → _____

다음은 Sally의 일기입니다. 일기를 읽고 질문에 답해 보세요.

bus stop 버스 정류장
lunch box 도시락
zoo 동물원

I got up early this morning. I went to the bus stop with a lunch box and meet Mary there. We took a bus and go to the zoo. I took 30 minutes to the zoo. We liked monkeys. We run to the monkeys first. We ate lunch on the bench. We saw many animals and took pictures. We had a great day.

1 Find and circle the three incorrect words. Then rewrite the words below.

→ _____ _____ _____

2 Did Sally met Mary at the zoo?

→ ☐ Yes, _____. ☐ No, _____.

3 Did Sally and Mary go to the zoo?

→ ☐ Yes, _____. ☐ No, _____.

4 Did Sally and Mary see the lions first?

→ ☐ Yes, _____. ☐ No, _____.

5 Did they eat lunch at the restaurant?

→ ☐ Yes, _____. ☐ No, _____.

6 Did Sally have a good time today?

→ ☐ Yes, _____. ☐ No, _____.

[1~2] 다음 중 빈칸에 알맞은 것을 고르세요.

1 He and she _____ late then.
① is ② are ③ was ④ were

2 Her birthday _____ yesterday.
① isn't   ② wasn't
③ don't   ④ didn't

3 다음 중 빈칸에 was를 쓸 수 <u>없는</u> 것을 고르세요.
① It _____ a nice dinner.
② John _____ sick last night.
③ The soldiers _____ kind.
④ The show _____ interesting.

[4~5] 다음 밑줄 친 부분 중 어법상 <u>어색한</u> 것을 고르세요.

4 ① My brother ② go ③ to a ④ boys' high school last year.

5 His parents ① don't ② have ③ a beautiful ④ garden at that time.

6 다음 빈칸에 들어갈 말이 알맞게 짝지어진 것을 고르세요.

> My sister _____ short last year, but she _____ tall now.

① is – was   ② was – was
③ was – is   ④ were – are

7 다음 대화의 빈칸에 들어갈 말을 쓰세요.

> A: _____ you late for school yesterday?
> B: No, I _____ .

_____ _____

[8~9] 다음 중 밑줄 친 부분의 쓰임이 <u>잘못된</u> 것을 고르세요.

8 ① Yesterday she <u>did</u> the dishes.
② He <u>didn't</u> like baseball.
③ I <u>buy</u> food at the market then.
④ They <u>answered</u> kindly to her.

9 ① That <u>wasn't</u> her bag.
② I <u>spoke</u> French well at that time.
③ Our house <u>were</u> very clean.
④ We <u>didn't</u> have breakfast yesterday.

[10~12] 다음 중 올바른 문장을 고르세요.

10 ① Were you sick yesterday?
② Did he went to the hospital?
③ Were your sister angry?
④ Did he swims in the river?

11 ① Your friends was very kind.
② He didn't understands that.
③ Jane slept well on the bed.
④ She did not came to school.

12
① I wasn't finish the work.
② I go to the museum yesterday.
③ We was not ten years old.
④ They didn't wait for me there.

13 다음 우리말과 같은 뜻이 되도록 빈칸에 알맞은 말을 쓰세요.

> 우리는 어젯밤에 야구 경기를 보았다. 그 경기는 재미있지 않았다.
> = We watched a baseball game last night. The game _____ _____ interesting.

_____ _____

14 다음 중 밑줄 친 부분을 축약형으로 잘못 바꾼 것을 고르세요.
① I did not live in New York last year.
→ didn't
② Adam and Dan were not at the station. → were't
③ Jonathan was not afraid of cats then. → wasn't
④ Julia does not read a newspaper.
→ doesn't

[15~16] 다음 문장에서 **틀린** 부분을 바르게 고쳐 쓰세요.

15 Brian and Judy was hungry then.

_____ → _____

16 Did she went to the bank yesterday?

_____ → _____

[17~18] 다음 중 질문에 대한 대답으로 알맞은 것을 고르세요.

17
> A: Did Mr. Smith go to the beach last summer?
> B: _____

① Yes, he was.   ② Yes, he does.
③ No, he didn't.   ④ No, he did.

18
> A: Were you interested in collecting coins?
> B: _____

① Yes, I were.   ② Yes, I was.
③ No, I didn't.   ④ No, I am not.

[19~20] 다음 문장을 지시대로 잘 바꾼 것을 고르세요.

19 We lose the game. (과거 부정문)
① We lost the game.
② We didn't lose the game.
③ We don't lose the game.
④ We weren't lose the game.

20 He builds the house. (과거 의문문)
① He didn't built the house?
② Does he build the house?
③ Did he build the house?
④ Did he built the house?

 서술형 평가

A 다음 밑줄 친 동사를 이용하여 빈칸에 알맞은 말을 쓰세요.

1 The children __liked__ fun TV shows.

They _____ comedy shows. But they _____ _____ news programs.

2 The first train __leaves__ at six a.m.

But this morning, it _____ _____ at six a.m. It _____ at six fifteen.

B 다음 그림을 보고, 질문에 알맞은 답을 쓰세요.

1 〈보기〉 단어들을 이용하여 주어 I로 시작하는 과거형 문장을 만드세요.

> 〈보기〉 visit, eat, swim, yesterday, a few days ago, last weekend

- _____
- _____
- _____

2 완성한 과거형 문장을 부정문으로 만드세요.

- _____
- _____
- _____

134 · Unit 6

Unit 7

과거진행형

과거진행형의 의미와 쓰임을 이해할 수 있다.

진행형을 쓸 수 없는 동사의 종류를 알 수 있다.

과거진행형의 부정문과 의문문을 이해하고 활용할 수 있다.

진행시제는 어떤 일이 일어나고 있는 중임을 나타내는 시제예요. 현재 진행형은 지금 어떤 일이 진행 중임을 나타내요. 과거진행형은 과거의 어느 시점에서 어떤 일이 일어나고 있던 중임을 나타낼 때 써요. 현재진행형은 '지금 ～하는 중이다'라는 뜻이고 과거진행형은 '～하고 있었던 중이다'라는 뜻이에요.

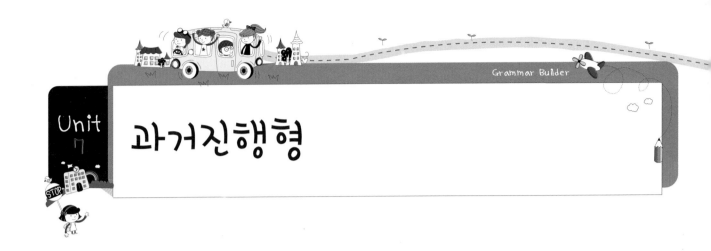

Unit 7

과거진행형

1. 과거진행형 문장

• 진행시제는 어떤 일이 일어나고 있는 중임을 나타내는 시제이다.

• 현재진행형은 지금 어떤 일이 진행 중임을 나타낸다. 과거진행형은 과거의 어느 시점에서 무슨 일이 일어나고 있던 중임을 나타낼 때 쓴다.

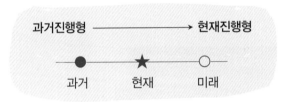

구분	형태	뜻
현재진행형	주어＋be동사(am, are, is)＋동사 -ing	~하는 중이다, ~하고 있다
과거진행형	주어＋be동사(was, were)＋동사 -ing	~하는 중이었다, ~하고 있었다

He was going to school. 그는 학교에 가고 있었다.
They were reading books. 그들은 책을 읽고 있었다.

주어에 따라 맞는 be동사를 쓴 후, 일반 동사의 원형에 -ing를 붙인다.

2. 진행형을 사용할 수 없는 동사

진행형은 행동이나 사건이 발생한 경우에 쓰기 때문에 소유나 상태를 나타내는 동사들은 진행형을 쓰지 않는다.

〈진행형 불가 동사〉

> · 소유: have(소유하다), belong(~에 속하다)
> · 상태: like(좋아하다), hate(싫어하다), want(원하다), know(알다)
> · 인지: understand(이해하다), remember(기억하다), resemble(닮다)

I have a book. 나는 책을 1권 가지고 있다.   I am having a book. (×)

He likes you. 그는 너를 좋아한다.   He is liking you. (×)

I am having lunch now. (○) 나는 지금 점심을 먹고 있다.

We are having a good time. (○) 나는 즐거운 시간을 보내고 있다.

have는 '먹다', 시간은 '보내다'의 경우에는 진행형이 가능하다.

Pop Quiz I. 다음 동사의 -ing형을 쓰세요.

❶ come → _____   ❷ study → _____   ❸ run → _____

3. 과거진행형의 부정문

과거진행형의 부정문은 be동사의 부정문을 만드는 법과 같다. be동사(was, were) 다음에 not을 써서 만든다.

형태	주어+be동사+not+동사의 -ing형	~하고 있지 않았다

We were watching a movie. 우리는 영화를 보고 있었다.

→ We were not watching a movie. 우리는 영화를 보고 있지 않았다.

He was reading books. 그는 책들을 읽고 있었다.

→ He was not reading books. 그는 책들을 읽고 있지 않았다.

4. 과거진행형의 의문문

과거진행형의 의문문은 be동사의 의문문 만드는 방법과 같은데, 주어와 be동사의 자리를 바꾸고
문장 끝에 물음표를 붙여서 만든다.

형태	be동사+주어+동사의 -ing형 ~?	~하고 있었니?

She was carrying a chair. 그녀는 의자를 나르고 있었다.

→ Was she carrying a chair? 그녀는 의자를 나르고 있었니?

   – Yes, she was. / No, she wasn't. 응, 그래. / 아니, 그렇지 않아.

They were playing soccer. 그들은 축구를 하고 있었다.

→ Are they playing soccer? 그들은 축구를 하고 있었니?

   – Yes, they were. / No, they weren't. 응, 그래. / 아니, 그렇지 않아.

대답은 be동사의
의문문과 같은 방법으로
'Yes/No'를 이용하여
답한다.

Pop Quiz

2. 다음 괄호 안에서 알맞은 것을 고르세요.

❶ Tom (were, was) sleeping.　❷ We (were, was) playing soccer.

be동사가 있는 모든 문장의 형태		
긍정문	주어+be동사 ~.	Ann is a teacher. Ann은 선생님이다.
부정문	주어+be동사+not ~.	Ann is not a teacher. Ann은 선생님이 아니다.
의문문	be동사+주어 ~?	Is Ann a teacher? Ann은 선생님이니?

다음 빈칸에 동사의 -ing형을 쓰세요.

1 jump _____

2 carry _____

3 come _____

4 build _____

5 play _____

6 read _____

7 run _____

8 take _____

9 write _____

10 see _____

11 ride _____

12 lie _____

13 sleep _____

14 climb _____

15 send _____

16 feel _____

17 study _____

18 plan _____

19 make _____

20 fall _____

21 walk _____

22 buy _____

23 die _____

24 say _____

25 cook _____

26 bring _____

27 listen _____

28 cut _____

29 eat _____

30 dance _____

다음 괄호 안에서 알맞은 것을 골라 동그라미 하세요.

bug 벌레
jeans 청바지
yard 마당
belong 소유이다

1 It was (snowing, snows) a lot.

2 He (were, was) catching some bugs.

3 She and he (were, was) wearing jeans.

4 We (had, was having) a beautiful yard.

5 Thomas was (help, helping) his father.

6 My uncles (was, were) reading newspapers.

7 This book (was belonging, belonged) to me.

8 The bird was (fliing, flying) up in the sky.

9 The girls were (play, playing) with the dolls.

10 Susan was (writeing, writing) a letter to me.

11 Jack (was, were) talking with his friends.

12 My brother and I (was, were) drinking milk.

13 We (was, were) singing the song.

14 My son (was remembering, remembered) you.

15 He was (swiming, swimming) in the lake.

16 They (were, was) carrying the furniture.

다음 주어진 단어를 이용하여 과거진행형 문장을 완성하세요.

rock 바위
snowman 눈사람
hill 언덕
truck 트럭

1 He _____ tennis with them. (play)

2 You _____ on a rock. (sit)

3 The children _____ snowmen. (make)

4 Sally _____ TV in the room. (watch)

5 He _____ the dishes after dinner. (do)

6 We _____ to the market. (go)

7 Ann and Sue _____ on the bed. (sleep)

8 I _____ to music on the sofa. (listen)

9 My dad _____ the living room. (clean)

10 They _____ their grandparents. (visit)

11 Tony _____ a new desk. (buy)

12 Mary and Dan _____ on the hill. (ski)

13 They _____ a great day. (have)

14 Jonathan _____ a truck. (drive)

15 Alice _____ to the park. (walk)

16 They _____ the problems. (solve)

다음 그림을 보고, 과거진행형 문장을 완성하세요.

draw 그림을 그리다

kite 연

1 Ann _____ on the bench. (sit)

2 Mark and Matt _____ in the park. (run)

3 Jill _____ with her dog. (walk)

4 Sally _____ a song. (sing)

5 Tom _____ the guitar. (play)

6 Brian _____ a bike. (ride)

7 Alice and Dan _____ a picture. (draw)

8 Chris and Jack _____ soccer. (play)

9 Eric _____ a kite on the hill. (fly)

10 They _____ a good time. (have)

다음 과거 문장을 과거진행형 문장으로 바꿔 다시 쓰세요.

1 My father drove to the market.

→ _____

2 Amy read the guidebook.

→ _____

3 The people brought a lot of silver.

→ _____

4 The students solved the easy problem.

→ _____

5 The rain fell heavily from the sky.

→ _____

6 We caught the dragonfly.

→ _____

7 The kangaroo jumped high.

→ _____

8 The soccer player kicked the ball.

→ _____

9 It snowed a lot in New York.

→ _____

10 They ate some bread for lunch.

→ _____

guidebook 안내서
silver 은
dragonfly 잠자리
player 운동선수

다음 문장을 과거진행형의 부정문으로 바꿔 다시 쓰세요.

gym 체육관
hotel 호텔
lemonade 레모네이드
dig 파다
language 언어

1 Nick exercised at the gym.

→ _____

2 They lied to their parents.

→ _____

3 The men stayed at the hotel.

→ _____

4 Judy drank lemonade.

→ _____

5 You dug a big hole.

→ _____

6 I read a novel at that time.

→ _____

7 We stood in front of the door.

→ _____

8 Cathy studied two languages.

→ _____

9 The children had lunch.

→ _____

10 He used the Internet.

→ _____

다음 문장을 과거진행형 의문문으로 바꾸고 대답도 바르게 완성하세요.

bark 짖다
shower 샤워
donut 도넛

1 The dog was barking at him.

→ _____ – Yes, _____

2 They were building a castle.

→ _____ – No, _____

3 Birds were flying to the south.

→ _____ – Yes, _____

4 You were doing your best.

→ _____ – Yes, _____

5 Tom was taking a shower.

→ _____ – No, _____

6 Sally was cutting the cake.

→ _____ – Yes, _____

7 Kevin was riding a bicycle.

→ _____ – No, _____

8 Dan and Ann were selling donuts.

→ _____ – Yes, _____

9 She was sleeping on the sofa.

→ _____ – No, _____

10 Dorothy was singing a song.

→ _____ – Yes, _____

다음 빈칸에 알맞은 말을 쓰세요.

1 _____시제는 어떤 일이 일어나고 있는 중임을 나타내는 시제로 _____진행형은 과거의 어느 시점에서 어떤 일이 일어나고 있던 중임을 나타낼 때 쓴다.

구분	형태	뜻
현재진행형	주어+be동사(____, ____, ____)+동사 -ing형	~하고 있다, ~하는 중이다
_____진행형	주어+be동사(was, ____)+동사 -ing형	~하고 있었다, ~하는 중이었다

2 **진행형 불가 동사**

- 소유: have(소유하다), _____(~에 속하다)
- 상태: like(좋아하다), _____(싫어하다), want(원하다), _____(알다)
- 인지: understand(이해하다), _____(기억하다), resemble(닮다)

3 과거진행형의 부정문은 be동사(_____, _____) 다음에 _____을 써서 만든다.

형태	주어+be동사+_____+동사의 -_____형	~하고 있지 않았다

4 과거진행형의 의문문은 _____와 _____동사의 자리를 바꾸고 문장 끝에 물음표를 붙여서 만든다.

형태	_____동사+_____+동사의 -ing형 ~?	~하고 있었니?

※대답은 be동사의 의문문과 같은 방법으로 _____나 _____를 이용하여 답한다.

be동사가 있는 모든 문장의 형태		
긍정문	주어+be동사 ~.	Ann is a teacher. Ann은 선생님이다.
부정문	주어+be동사+not ~.	Ann is not a teacher. Ann은 선생님이 아니다.
의문문	be동사+주어 ~?	Is Ann a teacher? Ann은 선생님이니?

다음 문장을 지시대로 올바르게 바꿔 다시 쓰세요.

1 They talk with their teacher. (과거진행형 긍정문)

→ _____

2 The player kicks the ball. (과거진행형 부정문)

→ _____

3 I touch the china. (과거진행형 부정문)

→ _____

4 He cooks in the kitchen. (과거진행형 의문문)

→ _____

5 Peter laughs at me. (과거진행형 긍정문)

→ _____

6 Joseph sends a text message. (과거진행형 의문문)

→ _____

7 We wait for Susie. (과거진행형 부정문)

→ _____

8 He listens to the radio. (과거진행형 부정문)

→ _____

9 My son puts forks on the table. (과거진행형 긍정문)

→ _____

10 His mother buys many things. (과거진행형 의문문)

→ _____

china 도자기
kitchen 부엌
laugh 웃다
text 본문, 문서
fork 포크

다음 빈칸에 알맞은 동사를 골라 과거진행형 문장을 완성하세요.

〈보기〉	help	play	fly	write	swim	study
	watch	have	sing	carry	come	hug

1 Brian _____ a movie at the theater.

2 The birds _____ to the north.

3 Billy _____ baseball on the playground.

4 Some children _____ in the river.

5 Jane and Dan _____ the bags.

6 She _____ a song in front of her family.

7 The students _____ lunch together.

8 Jerry _____ many poor people.

9 The boy _____ a letter to his parents.

10 He _____ to my office with his wife.

11 We _____ hard for the test.

12 The little kid _____ the teddy bear.

together 함께

office 사무실

hug 껴안다

다음 문장에서 틀린 부분에 ×표하고 바르게 고쳐 빈칸에 쓰세요.

pet 애완동물
resemble 닮다
number 수, 번호

1 Her sister were wearing a blouse.   → _____

2 They wasn't talking about you.   → _____

3 We were takeing care of your dogs.   → _____

4 Dorothy was knowing Mark.   → _____

5 Was he writing a letter? – Yes, he did. → _____

6 John not was doing his homework.   → _____

7 They were having a lot of pets.   → _____

8 Her brother weren't cutting the cake. → _____

9 Was Sue and Tom drinking coffee?   → _____

10 He was cookking Italian food there.   → _____

11 Mary and her sister was selling rings. → _____

12 Thomas is resembling his father.   → _____

13 Was it snowing a lot? – No, it weren't. → _____

14 Was you looking at me then?   → _____

15 She were not jumping on the bed.   → _____

16 We was remembering his car number. → _____

[1~2] 다음 중 동사와 -ing형이 바르게 짝지어 진 것을 고르세요.

1
① turn – turnning
② come – comeing
③ die – dying
④ hit - hiting

2
① arrive – arriveing
② run – running
③ plant – plantting
④ lie – lieing

3 다음 중 동사와 -ing형이 <u>잘못</u> 짝지어진 것을 <u>고르세요</u>.
① read – reading
② sit – sitting
③ watch – watching
④ ride – rideing

[4~5] 다음 빈칸에 들어갈 말로 알맞은 것을 고르세요.

4 This building _____ a soccer ball.
① resemble
② resembles
③ is resembling
④ was resembling

5 She was _____ a walk with her dog.
① take   ② takes
③ taking   ④ took

[6~7] 다음 우리말과 같도록 빈칸에 알맞은 말을 쓰세요.

6 Mary와 Tony는 숲 속을 걷고 있었다.
→ Mary and Tony _____ _____ in the forest.

7 그녀는 빨간 드레스를 입고 있었다.
→ She _____ _____ a red dress.

[8~9] 다음 대화의 빈칸에 알맞은 대답을 고르세요.

8
> A: Was it snowing a lot?
> B: _____

① Yes, it was.   ② Yes, it is.
③ No, it weren't.   ④ No, it isn't.

9
> A: Was Sally helping your work?
> B: _____

① Yes, she is.
② Yes, she did.
③ No, she wasn't.
④ No, she didn't.

10 다음 빈칸에 was[Was]를 쓸 수 <u>없는</u> 것을 고르세요.
① Jonathan _____ not fat.
② Tom and Ann _____ my students.
③ _____ Mr. Brown in Europe?
④ _____ the problem difficult?

11 다음 중 빈칸에 들어갈 알맞은 말을 고르세요.

> He _____ a good house then.

① has　　　② have
③ had　　　④ was having

12 다음 중 빈칸에 공통으로 알맞은 말을 고르세요.

> She _____ very sick yesterday.
> He _____ taking a math test.

① is　　　② are
③ was　　　④ were

13 다음 중 밑줄 친 부분이 올바른 것을 고르세요.

① Peter was <u>winning</u> the game now.
② The driver was <u>drive</u> the bus.
③ They are <u>liking</u> to ask questions.
④ We were <u>climbing</u> the mountain.

[14~15] 다음 중 바르지 않은 문장을 고르세요.

14 ① It was raining a lot.
② You were sitting on my seat.
③ They weren't doing the work.
④ My uncle were painting his wall.

15 ① Jim and I was playing soccer.
② I was using the blue marker.
③ He remembered her address.
④ We were having dinner there.

16 다음 우리말과 같도록 주어진 단어들을 바르게 배열하세요.

> 그들은 점심 식사 후에 조깅을 하고 있지 않았다.
> (jogging, they, after lunch, not, were)

→ _____

[17~18] 다음 문장을 지시대로 바꿔 쓰세요.

17 My cat slept on the sofa.
(과거진행형 부정문)
→ _____

18 Her son brushes his teeth.
(과거진행형 의문문)
→ _____

[19~20] 지금 시각은 오후 5시입니다. 다음 표를 보고, 문장을 완성하세요.

	1:00~2:00 p.m.	4:00~4:50
Bill	have lunch	read a novel
Judy, Lisa	play the piano	do their homework

19 Bill _____ from 1:00~2:00 p.m.

20 Judy and Lisa _____
from 4:00~4:50 p.m.

A 다음 그림을 보고, 빈칸에 알맞은 말을 쓰세요.

two hours ago

now

1 What was the boy doing two hours ago?

– He _____ _____ a bike in the park.

2 What is the boy doing now?

– He _____ _____ the violin in the living room.

B 다음 Sally의 오후 일과표를 보고, 빈칸에 알맞은 말을 쓰세요.

4:30~5:30	do her homework	
5:30~6:30	watch TV with her sister	7:50
6:30~7:30	have dinner with her family	
7:30~8:00	take a walk in the park	now

1 At 5:15, Sally _____ _____ her homework.

2 At 6:00, Sally _____ _____ _____ with her sister.

3 At 7:10, she _____ _____ _____ with her family.

4 Now, Sally _____ _____ a walk in the park.

Unit 8

동사의 미래시제

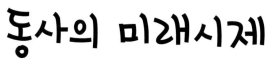

동사의 미래시제의 의미와 쓰임을 이해할 수 있다.

will을 이용하여 미래시제를 만들 수 있다.

be going to를 이용하여 미래시제를 만들 수 있다.

미래시제는 앞으로 일어날 일이나 계획을 나타낼 때 사용하는데, 동사의 미래형을 이용해서 나타내요. 미래형 문장을 나타낼 때는 조동사 will이나 be going to를 동사 앞에 붙여서 만들며 '~일 것이다', '~할 것이다'라는 뜻이에요.

Unit 8

동사의 미래시제

1. 미래형 문장

앞으로 일어날 일이나 계획, 의지를 나타낼 때 미래형 문장으로 나타낸다.
미래형 문장을 나타낼 때는 조동사 will이나 be going to를 동사 앞에
붙여서 만들며 '~일 것이다', '~할 것이다'라는 뜻이다.

주어가 3인칭 단수
일지라도 will이나
be going to 다음에는
반드시 동사원형을
써야 한다.

〈현재〉 He buys a computer. 그는 컴퓨터를 산다.

〈미래〉 He will buy a computer. 그는 컴퓨터를 살 것이다.

　　　He wills buy a computer. (×) / He will buys a computer. (×)

> **미래를 나타내는 말**
>
> tomorrow 내일, the day after tomorrow 모레, next week 다음 주, next month 다음 달,
> next year 내년, soon 곧, some day 언젠가

2. will을 이용한 미래형 문장

조동사 will은 예상, 의지, 추측을 나타낼 때 사용한다. will을 이용한 문장은 will+동사원형의 형
태로 나타내며 will은 주어와 함께 축약형으로 쓰이기도 한다.

I will[I'll] go there tomorrow. 나는 내일 그곳에 갈 것이다. 〈will의 축약형〉

> I will → I'll, You will → You'll, He will → He'll, She will → She'll, It will → It'll,
> We will → We'll, They will → They'll

(1) 부정문 ▷ Unit 4 참고

조동사의 부정문 만드는 방법과 같다. will 뒤에 not을 붙여서 만든다.

He <u>will not</u> buy a computer.(=won't) 그는 컴퓨터를 사지 않을 것이다.

(2) 의문문 ▷ Unit 4 참고

주어와 will의 위치를 바꾸고 문장 끝에 물음표를 붙이면 된다. 대답은 Yes나 No를 사용하여 나타낸다.

Will he buy a computer? 그는 컴퓨터를 살 거니?

– Yes, he will. (긍정) / – No, he won't. (부정)

> **Pop Quiz**
>
> 1. 다음 괄호 안에서 알맞은 것을 고르세요.
>   ❶ It will (be, is) snow soon.   ❷ He will (go, goes) there.

3. be going to를 이용한 미래형 문장

be going to 다음에는 동사원형이 오며 계획되어 있는 미래의 일을 나타낼 때 사용한다. be동사에는 주어에 맞게 am, are, is를 쓴다.

He <u>is going to</u> meet her.(=will) 그는 그녀를 만날 것이다.

It <u>will</u> rain soon.(=is going to) 곧 비가 올 것이다.

I <u>will</u> be 9 years old next year.(≠am going to) 내년에 9살이 될 것이다.

객관적인 사실을 말할때는 보통 be going to를 사용하지 않는다.

(1) 부정문 ▷ 1권 – Unit 8 참고

be동사의 부정문을 만드는 방법처럼 be동사 뒤에 not만 붙이면 된다.

He <u>is not</u> going to meet her.(=isn't) 그는 그녀를 만나지 않을 것이다.

(2)의문문 ▷ 1권 – Unit 8 참고

be동사의 의문문을 만드는 방법과 같은데, 주어와 be동사의 위치를 바꾸고 문장 끝에 물음표를 붙인다. 대답은 Yes나 No를 사용하여 나타낸다.

Is he going to meet her tomorrow? 그는 내일 그녀를 만날 거니?

– Yes, he is. (긍정) / No, he isn't. (부정)

	will을 이용한 문장	be going to를 이용한 문장
부정문	주어＋will＋not＋동사원형	주어＋am[are, is]＋not＋going to＋동사원형
의문문	will＋주어＋동사원형 ~?	Am[Are, Is]＋주어＋going to＋동사원형 ~?

4. 미래를 표현하는 다른 방법

왕래발착(가다, 오다, 출발하다, 도착하다) 동사는 현재시제로 정해지고 계획된 미래의 일을 나타낼 수 있다.

→ 왕래발착 동사: go, come, leave, start, arrive

He leaves for Seoul tomorrow. 그는 내일 서울로 떠난다.

> **Pop Quiz**
> **2.** 다음 괄호 안에서 알맞은 것을 고르세요.
> · She is going to (meet, meeting, meets) him tomorrow.

다음 괄호 안에서 알맞은 것을 고르세요.

rest 휴식

invite 초대하다

dentist 치과의사

1 She and he will (listens, listen) to the radio.

2 My brother (wills, will) go to the airport.

3 Sally (am, is, are) going to sing a song.

4 Eric (will, wills) (play, plays) soccer.

5 The man will (hunt, hunting) the tiger.

6 It will (is, be) Thursday tomorrow.

7 Tom is going to (take, takes) a rest here.

8 Judy (be, is) going to (wash, washes) her face.

9 She (will, is going to) be 11 years old next year.

10 John (will, wills) (invite, invites) his friends.

11 He will (is, be, was) a good dentist.

12 We are going to (meet, met) Ann in the park.

13 The farmer (will, wills) plant the flowers.

14 She (is, be) going to (buys, buy) a bike.

15 They (are, is, be) going to ride the horses.

16 The kids will (flew, fly) the kites on the hill.

다음 두 문장의 뜻이 같도록 빈칸에 알맞은 말을 올바르게 쓰세요.

arrive 도착하다
barbecue 바비큐
land 착륙하다
order 주문하다

1 She will arrive here tomorrow.

= She _____ _____ _____ _____ here tomorrow.

2 They are going to send a gift to her.

= They _____ _____ a gift to her.

3 Sarah and I will help our teacher.

= Sarah and I _____ _____ _____ _____ our teacher.

4 I will start this work next week.

= I _____ _____ _____ _____ this work next week.

5 We are going to have a barbecue party.

= We _____ _____ a barbecue party.

6 The plane will land in Seoul.

= The plane _____ _____ _____ _____ in Seoul.

7 They are going to move next month.

= They _____ _____ next month.

8 Bill is going to travel to London next year.

= Bill _____ _____ to London next year.

9 He will order many books tonight.

= He _____ _____ _____ _____ many books tonight.

10 I will play computer games soon.

= I _____ _____ _____ _____ computer games soon.

다음 빈칸에 알맞은 말을 넣어 미래형 문장을 올바르게 완성하세요.

warm 따뜻한
attend 참석하다
carpenter 목수

1 It _____ _____ warm next weekend. (be)

2 Her sister _____ _____ invitation cards. (make)

3 We _____ _____ _____ _____ a new dictionary. (buy)

4 Tony _____ _____ his grandparents next week. (visit)

5 My sister _____ _____ for New York tomorrow. (leave)

6 He _____ _____ _____ _____ the meeting. (attend)

7 Tom and Mark _____ _____ _____ _____ English. (learn)

8 The child _____ _____ a diary tonight. (write)

9 Susie _____ _____ thirteen years old next year. (be)

10 My father _____ _____ _____ _____ the dishes. (do)

11 We _____ _____ _____ _____ a movie next week. (see)

12 Thomas _____ _____ with his friends. (dance)

13 The carpenter _____ _____ a house here. (build)

14 Alice and Sue _____ _____ a subway. (take)

15 My family _____ _____ dinner at the restaurant. (eat)

16 Joan _____ _____ _____ her clothes tomorrow. (sell)

Check Up 4

다음 빈칸에 알맞은 말을 넣어 미래형 문장을 완성하세요.

light 전등
fire station 소방서
country 시골
barber 이발사

1 She _____ _____ his daughter to the station. (drive)

2 My mother _____ _____ care of the baby. (take)

3 We _____ _____ _____ _____ off the lights. (turn)

4 Joseph _____ _____ these cars next week. (wash)

5 We _____ _____ _____ _____ some milk. (drink)

6 I _____ _____ _____ _____ to the fire station. (walk)

7 Peter _____ _____ to her birthday party. (come)

8 It _____ _____ Saturday the day after tomorrow. (be)

9 They _____ _____ _____ _____ in a country. (live)

10 Jane _____ _____ science next week. (study)

11 My brother _____ _____ a great actor. (be)

12 Jonathan _____ _____ _____ _____ in his office. (stay)

13 The barber _____ _____ the man's hair soon. (cut)

14 Lisa _____ _____ _____ _____ him tomorrow. (call)

15 We _____ _____ in the swimming pool. (swim)

16 Josh _____ _____ Matt's computer next week. (fix)

160 · Unit 8

다음 문장을 부정문으로 바꾸어 다시 쓰세요.

fine 맑은, 좋은
paint 칠하다
surprised 놀란
wine 포도주

1 It will be fine tomorrow.

→ _____

2 We are going to get there by subway.

→ _____

3 He is going to use much water.

→ _____

4 Kate and Ann will have oranges.

→ _____

5 I will be twelve years old next year.

→ _____

6 She is going to paint the house soon.

→ _____

7 They will be surprised at the news.

→ _____

8 I am going to watch a movie tonight.

→ _____

9 Sam is going to go to the concert.

→ _____

10 Jess will bring some wine next week.

→ _____

다음 문장을 의문문으로 바꾸어 다시 쓰세요.

end 끝나다

truth 진실

chance 기회

1 The class is going to end in ten minutes.

→ _____

2 Kate and Jill will like the presents.

→ _____

3 She will tell him about the truth.

→ _____

4 Lisa is going to be angry at her sister.

→ _____

5 Joe will help you with your homework.

→ _____

6 Tom's father will give him a chance.

→ _____

7 John is going to have a party.

→ _____

8 He will visit his uncle next month.

→ _____

9 Bob and Tom are going to stay at the hotel.

→ _____

10 She will buy a new chair next weekend.

→ _____

Step 2 — Build Up 1

다음 문장을 be going to를 사용하여 다시 쓰세요.

1 He will cook dinner for you.

→ _____

2 They will stay in Jeju for a week.

→ _____

3 She will follow the rules.

→ _____

4 Alex will join the club.

→ _____

5 I will finish the work soon.

→ _____

6 Sally will be in her room.

→ _____

7 My mother will visit my aunt soon.

→ _____

8 I will meet her in the department store.

→ _____

9 Sam will build the sand castle there.

→ _____

10 You will save money for his birthday.

→ _____

follow 따르다
join 가입하다
department store 백화점
sand 모래

다음 괄호 안의 말을 이용하여 미래형 문장을 올바르게 만드세요.

trip 여행
coat 코트
bake ~을 굽다

1 She brings you the ball. (will)

→ _____

2 I take a trip. (be going to)

→ _____

3 Tom and his sister draw pictures. (will)

→ _____

4 The woman makes some cookies. (will)

→ _____

5 He takes off his coat. (be going to)

→ _____

6 We bake some bread. (be going to)

→ _____

7 My mother cleans up my room. (will)

→ _____

8 He waits for you in front of the bank. (will)

→ _____

9 I read books in my room. (be going to)

→ _____

10 Jenny does her homework. (be going to)

→ _____

Build Up 3

다음 괄호 안의 말과 will을 이용하여 미래형 문장을 바르게 만드세요.

high school 고등학교
picnic 소풍
clearly 명확히

1 We go to see a movie. (tomorrow)

→ _____

2 My brother is a high school student. (next month)

→ _____

3 I can travel around the world. (some day)

→ _____

4 She buys an expensive car. (next week)

→ _____

5 His father comes back home. (soon)

→ _____

6 The woman leaves this country. (next year)

→ _____

7 Ann and Eric move to Paris. (tomorrow)

→ _____

8 Sally and Lisa meet at the bookstore. (next time)

→ _____

9 They go on a picnic to the river. (next week)

→ _____

10 We can see the star clearly. (tomorrow)

→ _____

다음 빈칸에 알맞은 말을 쓰세요.

1 미래형 문장을 나타낼 때는 조동사 _____이나 _____ _____ _____를 동사 앞에 붙여서 만들며 '~일 것이다', '~할 것이다'라는 뜻이다.

주어가 3인칭 단수일지라도 _____이나 _____ _____ _____ 다음에는 반드시 _____을 써야 한다.

2 **미래를 나타내는 말**

tomorrow 내일, the _____ _____ tomorrow 모레, next _____ 다음 주, next month 다음 달, _____ year 내년, _____ 곧, some day 언젠가

3 조동사 will은 주어와 함께 축약형으로 쓰이기도 한다.

I will → _____, You will → _____, He will → _____, She will → _____, It will → _____, We will → _____, They will → _____

4 조동사 will은 be going to로 바꾸어 쓸 수 있으며, will이 있는 미래형 문장의 부정문은 will 뒤에 _____을 붙여서 만든다. 의문문은 주어와 _____의 위치를 바꾸고 문장 끝에 물음표를 붙이면 된다.

5 be going to를 이용한 미래형 문장에서 be동사는 _____에 따라 am, are, is를 쓰며 부정문은 be동사 뒤에 _____만 붙여 만든다. 의문문은 be동사의 의문문 만드는 방법과 같은데, _____와 be동사의 위치를 바꾸고 문장 끝에 물음표를 붙인다.

6 _____ 동사는(가다, 오다, 출발하다, 도착하다를 나타내는 동사 - go, come, leave, start, arrive 등) _____시제로 정해지고 계획된 미래의 일을 나타낼 수 있다.

다음 문장을 괄호 안의 단어와 지시대로 바꾸어 올바르게 쓰세요.

musician 음악가
sandwich 샌드위치

1 He is a famous musician. (will, 긍정문)

→ _____

2 Sally wears a pink dress. (be going to, 부정문)

→ _____

3 She walks to the station. (will, 부정문)

→ _____

4 Eric exercises at the gym. (be going to, 긍정문)

→ _____

5 Jane makes sandwiches. (will, 부정문)

→ _____

6 My father fixes the door. (be going to, 부정문)

→ _____

7 We remember Sue's address. (will, 긍정문)

→ _____

8 Tommy passes the exam. (be going to, 긍정문)

→ _____

9 It rains a lot. (will, 부정문)

→ _____

10 My mother closes the window. (be going to, 부정문)

→ _____

다음 문장을 의문문으로 바꾸고 대답도 알맞게 완성하세요.

job 직업
disappear 사라지다
life 삶, 생명

1 They will lend their houses.

→ _____ – Yes, _____

2 He is going to have a job.

→ _____ – Yes, _____

3 The cat will live in your house.

→ _____ – No, _____

4 She will disappear after the show.

→ _____ – Yes, _____

5 Kate is going to came back soon.

→ _____ – No, _____

6 Tony and Judy will study hard.

→ _____ – Yes, _____

7 He is going to enjoy his life.

→ _____ – No, _____

8 They are going to play soccer.

→ _____ – Yes, _____

9 The train will arrive in ten minutes.

→ _____ – No, _____

10 Tom and Jane will go there.

→ _____ – Yes, _____

다음 문장에서 틀린 부분에 ×표하고 바르게 고쳐 빈칸에 쓰세요.

report 보고서
scarf 스카프
hometown 고향

1 She will helps me with my report. → _____

2 I will not played computer games. → _____

3 Will he stays with you this winter? → _____

4 Susan are going to buy this scarf. → _____

5 I will going back to my hometown. → _____

6 I am going to moving next month. → _____

7 My mom and dad will walks to the park. → _____

8 They are going of go to the zoo. → _____

9 Will she lends her bike next week? → _____

10 Brian will drinks some milk soon. → _____

11 They are going not to clean the room. → _____

12 The baby wills play with toys there. → _____

13 She is going to be six years old next year. → _____

14 Peter are going to write a letter tomorrow. → _____

15 Is his brother going to rides a bike? → _____

16 I will kicking the ball this afternoon. → _____

[1~2] 다음 문장에서 not이 들어가기에 알맞은 곳을 고르세요.

1 They ① are ② going ③ to ④ play baseball.

2 I ① will ② start ③ this homework ④ soon.

[3~4] 다음 중 빈칸에 알맞은 것을 고르세요.

3 John and Susie _____ at the bus stop in ten minutes.
① arrives
② arriving
③ arrived
④ will arrive

4 My family will eat dinner at the restaurant _____.
① last night
② yesterday
③ next week
④ ago

[5~6] 다음 중 밑줄 친 부분이 잘못된 것을 고르세요.

5 ① She is going to do the dishes.
② He leaves for Seoul tomorrow.
③ They will moves next month.
④ Sarah and I will help our teacher.

6 ① Ann will have oranges.
② We will won't bring some wine.
③ It won't be fine tomorrow.
④ I am not going to watch a movie.

7 다음 중 대화의 빈칸에 알맞은 것을 고르세요.

> A: _____ on the bed?
> B: No, I won't. I will study in my room.

① Will you sleep
② Do you sleep
③ Did you sleep
④ Were you sleeping

[8~9] 다음 의문문에 대한 대답으로 알맞은 것을 고르세요.

8 Will Tom's father give him a gift?
① Yes, he will.
② No, he isn't.
③ No, he will.
④ Yes, he is.

9 Is Jill going to have a party?
① Yes, she will.
② Yes, she does.
③ No, she isn't.
④ No, she won't.

10 다음 중 우리말을 영어로 바르게 옮긴 것을 고르세요.

> 그녀는 내일 그녀의 드레스를 입지 않을 것이다.

① She didn't wear her dress tomorrow.
② She will wear not her dress tomorrow.
③ She was not wearing her dress tomorrow.
④ She won't wear her dress tomorrow.

[11~13] 다음 중 바르지 않은 문장을 고르세요.

11 ① We are going to live here.
② The movie will end in ten minutes.
③ They were going to study tomorrow.
④ He will play the game next month.

12 ① We will meet the famous singer.
② Mark won't cleans his room.
③ I'm going to wash the dishes.
④ She is going to wait for him.

13 ① Sally will is in her room.
② He is going to take off his coat.
③ She will bring you the ball.
④ Joe is going to join the club.

14 다음 중 우리말과 같도록 주어진 단어를 바르게 배열한 것을 고르세요.

> Sue는 그들을 파티에 초대할 것이다.
> (the party, going to, Sue, them, to, is, invite)

① Sue is invite to them going to the party.
② Sue invite to them is going to the party.
③ Sue is going to invite them to the party.
④ Sue going to invite is them to the party.

15 다음 중 왕래발착 동사가 아닌 것을 고르세요.
① make ② come
③ arrive ④ leave

16 다음 각각의 빈칸에 동사 rain을 알맞은 형태로 쓰세요.
It _____ last month.
It is _____ in Seoul now.
It always _____ a lot here in summer.
It is going to _____ tomorrow.

[17~18] 다음에서 틀린 부분을 찾아 ○표 하고, 고쳐 문장을 다시 쓰세요.

17 His father will came back home soon.
→ _____

18 Tommy is going to passing the exam.
→ _____

[19~20] 다음 문장과 뜻이 같도록 빈칸에 알맞은 말을 쓰세요.

19 My uncle will exercise at the gym.
= My uncle ____ ____ ____ ____ at the gym.

20 Matt is not going to buy this sweater.
= Matt _____ _____ this sweater.

A 다음은 Alice 가족의 대화입니다. 10년 후의 모습에 관한 대화를 읽고, 질문에 답해 보세요.

> Father : I will not live in the city.
>   I am going to plant apple trees on the field.
> Mother : I will take a trip to Europe.
>   I am going to stay in France for a week.
> Brother : I will be a great soccer player.
>   I am going to win the World Cup.
> Alice   : I am good at singing.
>   I will be a famous singer.

1 Will Alice's father live in Seoul?

_____

2 Will Alice's brother be a great soccer player?

_____

3 Is Alice's mother going to stay in France?

_____

B 다음 그림을 보고, 대화의 빈칸에 알맞은 말을 쓰세요.

now   two hours later

1 What is he doing now?
  – He _____ in the swimming pool.

2 What is he going to do two hours later?
  – He _____ TV with his family.

Memo

1 다음 중 원급과 비교급의 짝이 바르지 않은 것을 고르세요.

① big – bigger
② cute – cuter
③ famous – famouser
④ happy – happier

[2~4] 다음 문장의 빈칸에 알맞은 말을 고르세요.

2 Jack is shorter _____ Mark.

① than   ② most
③ more   ④ as

3 Tom is the tallest _____ his class.

① of   ② as
③ than   ④ in

4 I need a pencil. Can you borrow _____?

① one   ② ones
③ it   ④ they

5 다음 문장과 의미가 같은 것을 고르세요.

> Sally is younger than Judy.

① Judy isn't older than Sally.
② Judy is older than Sally.
③ Sally is as old as Judy.
④ Judy is younger than Sally.

6 다음 중 인칭대명사와 재귀대명사의 짝이 바르지 않은 것을 고르세요.

① I – myself
② she – herself
③ they – theirselves
④ you – yourselves

7 다음 중 밑줄 친 부분이 어색한 것을 고르세요.

① Each student has a chair.
② Some friends live in Seoul.
③ One should do one's best.
④ All the kid have their own bike.

[8~10] 다음 밑줄 친 말과 바꿔 쓸 수 있는 것을 고르세요.

8 I will play soccer tomorrow.

① was going to ② is going to
③ am going to   ④ are going to

9 He must finish his homework.

① have to   ② has to
③ may not to   ④ may be

10 다음 중 숫자를 영어로 잘못 나타낸 것을 고르세요.

① 4.23 = four point two three
② ₩650 = six hundred and fifty wons
③ 2/5 = two fifths
④ $25.30 = twenty-five dollars thirty cents

11 다음 중 동사와 동사의 과거형이 바르지 <u>않은</u> 것을 고르세요.

① stop – stopped

② dance – danced

③ draw – drawed

④ carry – carried

12 다음 중 질문에 대한 대답으로 알맞은 것을 고르세요.

> Can you use a computer?

① Yes, I do.　　② Yes, I will.

③ No, I can.　　④ No, I can't.

13 다음 중 <u>어색한</u> 문장을 고르세요.

① It wasn't an airplane.

② She didn't get up at eight.

③ Was they study science hard?

④ Did you go to school yesterday?

[14~17] 다음 문장의 빈칸에 알맞은 것을 고르세요.

14 I _____ swim in the sea.

① can　　　② am

③ not　　　④ doesn't

15 She _____ be twelve years old next year.

① not　　　② don't

③ will　　　④ can

16 We _____ busy yesterday.

① is　　　② are

③ was　　　④ were

17 He _____ English at school three years ago.

① teached　　② taught

③ teaches　　④ teaching

[18~20] 다음 중 빈칸에 공통으로 들어갈 알맞은 것을 고르세요.

18
> · My father _____ a pilot then.
> · He _____ interested in photos.

① is　　　② are

③ was　　　④ were

19
> · _____ you have breakfast?
> · She _____ not come home early a few days ago.

① did　　　② don't

③ does　　　④ do

20
> · Two apples _____ on the table this morning.
> · _____ you sad yesterday?

① do　　　② were

③ was　　　④ did

1 다음 단어 중 성격이 <u>다른</u> 것을 고르세요.

① second　　② twelfth

③ hundredth　④ twenty

2 다음 중 숫자를 기수와 서수로 <u>잘못</u> 표기한 것을 고르세요.

① 3 – three – threeth

② 5 – five – fifth

③ 13 – thirteen – thirteenth

④ 40 – forty – fortieth

3 다음 두 단어의 관계가 나머지와 <u>다른</u> 것을 고르세요.

① many – more

② bad – worse

③ good – best

④ popular – more popular

4 다음 밑줄 친 부분을 의미가 같도록 다른 말로 쓰세요.

> She <u>can</u> help other people.

→ _____

5 다음 중 빈칸에 들어갈 알맞은 대명사를 고르세요.

> Jenny cut _____ with a knife.

① oneself　　② her

③ herself　　④ hers

6 다음 두 문장이 같은 의미가 되도록 빈칸에 들어갈 말을 고르세요.

> Math is not as interesting as science.
> = Science is _____ interesting than math.

① most　　② more

③ in　　　④ of

7 다음 중 밑줄 친 부분이 어색한 것을 고르세요.

① Every girl <u>likes</u> the singer.

② Each of us <u>knows</u> Madonna.

③ All of them <u>are</u> very diligent.

④ Both of the men <u>waits</u> for her.

[8~9] 다음 문장의 빈칸에 알맞은 것을 고르세요.

8 _____ of the boys has a robot.

① Each　　② Both

③ All　　　④ Every

9 He is the tallest _____ the six.

① than　　② as

③ in　　　④ of

10 다음 중 밑줄 친 부분과 바꿔 쓸 수 있는 것을 고르세요.

> You <u>must</u> go home now.

① have to　　② has to

③ may not　　④ are able to

11 다음 중 과거를 나타내는 말을 고르세요.

① tomorrow   ② next Sunday

③ last week   ④ soon

[12～13] 다음 빈칸에 공통으로 들어갈 알맞은 것을 고르세요.

12
> · They _____ be sleepy.
> · _____ I use your cell phone?

① can   ② may   ③ will   ④ do

13
> · The people _____ be Korean.
> · She is sick. She _____ go to see a doctor.

① will   ② don't

③ won't   ④ must

14 다음 문장에 will을 넣어 다시 쓴 문장이 바른 것을 고르세요.

> I can pass the exam.

① I will can pass the exam.

② I will able to pass the exam.

③ I will be able to pass the exam.

④ I will am able to pass the exam.

15 다음 중 동사와 동사의 과거형이 바르지 <u>않은</u> 것을 고르세요.

① eat – ate   ② think – thank

③ build – built   ④ buy – bought

16 다음 괄호 안의 단어를 빈칸에 알맞은 형태로 쓰세요.

Matt _____ pater in the park last weekend. (meet)

17 다음 문장을 부정문으로 바르게 고쳐 쓰세요.

> He saw her there.

→ _____

[18～19] 다음 중 빈칸에 공통으로 들어갈 알맞은 것을 고르세요.

18
> · I _____ a wallet last night.
> · The players _____ the game three days ago.

① won   ② lost

③ ate   ④ taught

19
> · She _____ come tomorrow.
> · Julie _____ be a teacher next month.

① will   ② be   ③ do   ④ did

20 다음 중 어색한 문장을 고르세요.

① He was doing the dishes.

② That wasn't his bag.

③ I went to the market then.

④ He was not buy a sweater.

초등 영어 교재의 베스트셀러

초등 영어 문법 실력 쌓기!

Grammar Builder

3

Answer Key

Answer Key

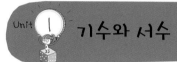

Unit 1 기수와 서수

Pop Quiz

1. ❶ second ❷ twelfth ❸ twentieth
2. ❶ eight point three five ❷ two thirds

■ **Step 1** | **Check Up 1**　　　　　　　p. 17

1. one, first **2.** three, third
3. five, fifth **4.** seven, seventh
5. nine, ninth **6.** eleven, eleventh
7. thirteen, thirteenth **8.** fifteen, fifteenth
9. seventeen, seventeenth
10. nineteen, nineteenth
11. twenty-one, twenty-first
12. twenty-three, twenty-third
13. thirty, thirtieth
14. fifty, fiftieth **15.** seventy, seventieth
16. one hundred, one hundredth

■ **Step 1** | **Check Up 2**　　　　　　　p. 18

1. two, second **2.** four, fourth **3.** six, sixth
4. eight, eighth **5.** ten, tenth **6.** twelve, twelfth
7. fourteen, fourteenth **8.** sixteen, sixteenth
9. eighteen, eighteenth **10.** twenty, twentieth
11. twenty-two, twenty-second
12. twenty-four, twenty-fourth **13.** forty, fortieth
14. sixty, sixtieth **15.** eighty, eightieth
16. one thousand, one thousandth

■ **Step 1** | **Check Up 3**　　　　　　　p. 19

1. nineteen eighty-four
2. June (the) fifteen(th)
3. nineteen ninety-one
4. May (the) four(th), two thousand
5. October (the) seven(th)
6. nineteen seventy
7. December (the) twenty-fifth, two thousand /
   December twenty-five, two thousand
8. thirteen fifty-two **9.** September (the) ten(th)
10. eighteen forty-five **11.** two thousand eight
12. April (the) second / April two
13. July (the) seven(th), two thousand twelve
14. May (the) fifth / May five **15.** twelve fifty-three
16. nineteen seventy-four

■ **Step 1** | **Check Up 4**　　　　　　　p. 20

1. five three eight four seven two five
2. three o four one two eight six
3. thirty-two dollars and twenty-five cents
4. seven hundred and fifty won
5. area code zero two, four nine two five two four
   seven
6. area code zero five three, two five eight one
   two eight four
7. fifty-eight dollars and fifteen cents
8. eighteen dollars and fifty-seven cents
9. five thousand, four hundred and ninety won
10. two eight four three six one four
11. eight five one two o four o
12. ninety-nine dollars and forty cents

13. nine thousand, nine hundred and ninety won

14. area code zero three one, two four one eight five o six

15. four hundred and forty dollars and ten cents

16. three three(double three) four one eight five two

■ Step 1 | Check Up 5   p. 21

1. two fifths 2. one third

3. seventy-five point two six

4. twelve point eight five four 5. five times

6. twice 7. five point zero seven

8. a quarter / one quarter 9. two and two thirds

10. ten times 11. three and three fourths

12. a half / one half 13. zero point two four

14. nine point nine nine 15. twelve times

16. four and one fifth

■ Step 1 | Check Up 6   p. 22

1. three eight two nine two o one

2. eighteen forty-five 3. twenty-fourth

4. forty-four point eight five 5. three sevenths

6. sixty-five dollars and twenty cents

7. eight dollars and seventy-five cents

8. August (the) fifteen(th)

9. nine hundred fifty won 10. three times

11. thirtieth 12. nine dollars and ten cents

13. two thousand, five hundred won

14. nineteen fifty

15. September (the) twenty-third(twenty-three)

16. nine eight five four one seven six

■ Step 2 | Build Up 1   p. 23

1. ten 2. the third 3. the fifth 4. The second

5. the sixth 6. nine 7. twelve 8. twice 9. eleven

10. the first 11. hundred 12. dollars 13. thirds

14. the fifth 15. the third 16. two

■ Step 2 | Build Up 2   p. 24

1. one 2. third 3. nine 4. four 5. ten 6. third

7. thirty 8. second 9. seventh 10. five

11. eighteen 12. sixth 13. fifty 14. three

15. sixty-three 16. twenty-fifth

■ Step 2 | Build Up 3   p. 25

1. second 2. four 3. seventh 4. forty-two

5. twelfth 6. two 7. fifth 8. ninth 9. eleven

10. sixth 11. thirtieth 12. one hundred 13. eight

14. third 15. thirteen 16. fourth

■ Step 3 | Jump 1   p. 26

1. first, second, third, fourth, fifth, sixth, seventh, eighth, ninth, tenth, eleventh, twelfth, thirteenth, fourteenth, fifteenth, nineteenth, twentieth, twenty-first, twenty-second, thirtieth, fortieth, ninetieth, one hundredth, one thousandth

2. 요일, 월, 년, 기수, 화폐, 기수, point, 기수, 서수, 복수형

■ Step 3 | Jump 2   p. 27

1. nineteen eighty-four 2. three fourths

3. two four six two one o three

4. thirty-five point nine nine

5. seventy-nine dollars seventy-eight cents

6. October (the) twenty-four(th)

7. seventeen twenty-eight

8. March sixteenth, two thousand

9. area code zero two, one four seven three two one five

10. two thousand, two hundred fifty won

■ Step 3 | Jump 3   p. 28

1. It is Jennifer's eighth novel.

2. They live on the fifteenth floor.

3. She is twelve years old.

4. This is a building of forty-five stories.

5. The fifth day of the week is Thursday.

6. There are thirty people on the playground.

7. Here is the fourth station from the gallery.

8. The third question is very difficult.

9. The bank is the seventh building on your right.

10. Judy sends ten letters to her friends.

■ Step 3 | Jump 4　　　　　　　　p. 29

1. fifth **2.** twelfth **3.** thirty **4.** second **5.** first

6. October **7.** twice **8.** tenth **9.** two

10. one, two, three

■ Step 4 | 실전 평가　　　　　　　　p. 30

1. ② **2.** ③ **3.** ④ **4.** ① **5.** three fifths **6.** ③ **7.** ②

8. ① **9.** ④ **10.** ③

11. three seven five two one four eight

12. area code zero two, eight six two nine three o seven

13. ② **14.** ② **15.** ③ **16.** ④ **17.** three times

18. fifteenth, June, nineteen sixty-nine

19. The seventh question is very easy.

20. I live in London for eight years.

1. eighteen은 기수이다.

2. 12의 서수는 twelfth이다.

3. 100의 서수는 one hundredth이다.

4. 2의 서수는 second이다.

5. 분자가 복수일 때는 분자를 복수로 나타낸다.

9. 두 번째를 나타내므로 the second라고 해야 한다.

10. 2배를 나타낼 때는 twice를 사용하며 3배 이상은 기수에 times를 붙여서 나타낸다.

11. 전화번호는 기수로 하나씩 읽는다.

14. 네 번째 책은 the fourth book, 방 3개는 three bedrooms이다.

15. 일주일에 두 번째 날은 the second day of the week이다

16. 63층 건물은 a building of sixty-three stories이다.

■ Step 5 | 서술형 평가　　　　　　　　p. 32

A first, third, fifth, sixth, eighth, tenth, twelfth

B **1.** a quarter **2.** a half **3.** three fourths
　4. one third

C **1.** seventh **2.** fifteen **3.** first

Unit ② 부정대명사, 재귀대명사

Pop Quiz

1. one
2. Both

■ Step 1 | Check Up 1　　　　　　　　p. 37

1. one **2.** it **3.** Some **4.** any **5.** Each **6.** Both

7. any **8.** All **9.** Each **10.** All **11.** Every **12.** One

13. one **14.** Both **15.** one **16.** All

■ Step 1 | Check Up 2　　　　　　　　p. 38

1. is **2.** are **3.** knows **4.** are **5.** likes **6.** are

7. student **8.** photo **9.** are **10.** Each **11.** Every

12. is **13.** others **14.** one **15.** the other

16. another, other

■Step 1 ı Check Up 3   p. 39

1. me 2. herself 3. himself 4. us 5. yourself
6. herself 7. themselves 8. himself
9. themselves 10. her 11. her 12. himself
13. me 14. herself 15. myself 16. ourselves

■Step 1 ı Check Up 4   p. 40

1. any 2. one 3. Some 4. themselves 5. Both
6. Each 7. ones 8. It 9. Every 10. has
11. himself 12. him 13. has 14. country 15. any
16. One, the other

■Step 1 ı Check Up 5   p. 41

1. some 2. it 3. one 4. another 5. any 6. one
7. Some 8. Another 9. It 10. Some 11. one
12. any

■Step 1 ı Check Up 6   p. 42

1. All 2. Each 3. other 4. Every 5. Both 6. All
7. Each 8. another 9. Both 10. Every 11. other
12. others

■Step 2 ı Build Up 1   p. 43

1. Some, others 2. another 3. Some 4. Every
5. one 6. Both 7. All 8. Each 9. One, the other
10. One, another, the other

■Step 2 ı Build Up 2   p. 44

1. Every 2. Each 3. myself 4. Both 5. another
6. ones 7. Some 8. All 9. One, the others
10. One, another, the other

■Step 2 ı Build Up 3   p. 45

1. himself 2. itself 3. yourselves 4. myself
5. themselves 6. yourself 7. herself 8. ourselves
9. myself 10. yourself 11. herself 12. yourselves

13. themselves 14. himself 15. themselves

■Step 3 ı Jump 1   p. 46

1. ones, one's, one, it 2. some, any, 복수, 단수
3. 단수, 복수, 사람, 단수, 단수, 단수
4. other, others, another, other 5. self, selves

■Step 3 ı Jump 2   p. 47

1. has 2. are 3. myself 4. some 5. man
6. another 7. the other 8. bags 9. myself
10. Some 11. others 12. themselves 13. is
14. books 15. another

■Step 3 ı Jump 3   p. 48

1. it 2. is 3. boys 4. are 5. ourselves 6. man
7. others 8. women 9. Every 10. yourself
11. One 12. Some 13. herself 14. man 15. other

■Step 3 ı Jump 4   p. 49

1. Every student has this book.
2. Each of the boys eats pizza.
3. All of the girls are very tall.
4. Some of the rooms are empty.
5. One should keep one's promise.
6. I want some cookies. Do you have any?
7. Both of the men play computer games.
8. Some like dogs, and others like cats.
9. One is mine, and the others are his.
10. One is pink, and the other is green.

■Step 4 ı 실전 평가   p. 50

1. ② 2. ③ 3. ③ 4. ④ 5. Each 6. themselves
7. ① 8. ① 9. ② 10. any 11. myself
12. computer 13. city, has 14. ① 15. ③ 16. ②
17. ④ 18. Both 19. herself

1. 앞에 나온 명사 fork와 같은 종류의 불특정한 것을 나타
   내므로 one이 와야 한다.
2. (둘 중) 하나는 ~이고 나머지 하나는 …라고 할 때
   One ~ and the other를 사용하여 나타낸다.
3. 몇몇은 ~이고 나머지는 …라고 할 때 Some ~
   others를 사용하여 나타낸다.
4. 재귀대명사는 주어 자신을 가리키는 말로 ④은 주어와
   다른 대상이므로 인칭대명사의 목적격인 you가 와야
   한다.
5. '품목의 각각은 가격표를 가지고 있다.'라는 뜻으로 각
   각에 해당하는 단어와 와야 한다.
6. 학생들 스스로 즐겼다는 뜻으로 주어에 해당하는 대상
   의 재귀대명사가 와야 한다.
8. 하나는 ~ 또 하나는 … 나머지는 …라는 뜻으로 셋을
   분류할 때는 one ~ another … the other …를 사용
   해서 나타낸다.
9. He is proud of 다음에는 him, himself, her가 들어
   갈 수 있는데, 두 번째 문장에서는 주어가 그 빵을 만
   든다고 해야 한다. 따라서 Brian의 재귀대명사인
   himself가 들어가야 한다.
10. some과 any는 '몇 개, 얼마, 어느 정도'라는 부정확
    한 수량을 나타낸다. some은 긍정문에, any는 부정
    문과 의문문에 쓰인다.
12. 앞에 나온 명사와 같은 종류의 불특정한 것을 나타내
    므로 여기서 one이 가리키는 것은 computer이다.
13. every는 '모든 ~'이라는 뜻으로 단독으로 쓰일 수
    없으며, 그 다음에 반드시 단수 명사가 오며 단수 취
    급한다.
14. each가 형용사로 쓰일 때는 each 다음에 단수명사
    가 온다. All 다음에 셀 수 있는 명사의 복수형이 오면
    복수 취급한다. 또한 every 다음에는 단수명사가 온
    다.
15. 긍정문에서는 any가 아닌 some을 쓴다. 문장에서
    each는 단수 취급하며 both는 복수 취급한다.
16. 불특정한 것을 가리킬 때는 it이 아닌 one을 사용하며
    one의 복수형은 ones이다.

■ **Step 5 | 서술형 평가**   p. 52

A 1. any 2. some
B 1. All, toys 2. Both, parents 3. Each, boxes
C 1. himself, herself 2. themselves

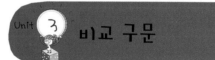

Unit 3 비교 구문

Pop Quiz

I. ❶ smaller, smallest ❷ bigger, biggest
2. ❶ than ❷ of

■ **Step 1 | Check Up 1**   p. 57

1. thinner, thinnest 2. less, least
3. shorter, shortest 4. bigger, biggest
5. larger, largest 6. more difficult, most difficult
7. more, most 8. older, oldest
9. prettier, prettiest 10. darker, darkest
11. cheaper, cheapest
12. more beautiful, most beautiful
13. faster, fastest 14. worse, worst
15. longer, longest 16. heavier, heaviest

■ **Step 1 | Check Up 2**   p. 58

1. busier, busiest 2. younger, youngest
3. happier, happiest 4. hotter, hottest

5. nicer, nicest 6. easier, easiest

7. more famous, most famous 8. smaller, smallest

9. better, best 10. worse, worst 11. more, most

12. more popular, most popular 13. wiser, wisest

14. better, best 15. taller, tallest 16. fatter, fattest

■ Step 1 | Check Up 3 p. 59

1. more, most 2. more special, most special

3. easier, easiest 4. stranger, strangest

5. happier, happiest

6. more popular, most popular 7. faster, fastest

8. drier, driest 9. stronger, strongest

10. lovelier, loveliest 11. worse, worst

12. higher, highest 13. bigger, biggest

14. less, least 15. shorter, shortest

16. more careful, most careful

■ Step 1 | Check Up 4 p. 60

1. hungrier, hungriest 2. better, best

3. more dangerous, most dangerous

4. hotter, hottest 5. more useful, most useful

6. prettier, prettiest 7. more, most

8. smarter, smartest 9. politer, politest

10. larger, largest 11. wetter, wettest

12. cuter, cutest

13. more handsome, most handsome

14. thinner, thinnest 15. angrier, angriest

16. cheaper, cheapest

■ Step 1 | Check Up 5 p. 61

1. strongest 2. smarter 3. busiest 4. faster

5. earlier 6. younger 7. happier 8. heavier

9. cutest 10. best 11. darker 12. bravest

13. famous 14. more 15. biggest 16. interesting

■ Step 1 | Check Up 6 p. 62

1. colder 2. smaller 3. bigger 4. more beautiful

5. most difficult 6. higher 7. largest 8. longer

9. cheaper 10. thicker 11. harder 12. oldest

13. more expensive 14. tallest 15. less

16. most dangerous

■ Step 2 | Build Up 1 p. 63

1. faster than 2. as popular as

3. more beautiful than 4. the highest

5. younger than 6. more boring than

7. as smart as 8. the most famous

9. not as sweet as 10. the best

■ Step 2 | Build Up 2 p. 64

1. the bravest 2. the best 3. colder than

4. the oldest 5. as quick as 6. the busiest

7. fatter than 8. as difficult as 9. the biggest

10. The worst

■ Step 2 | Build Up 3 p. 65

1. taller than 2. more expensive than

3. long as that ruler 4. the cheapest of

5. older than 6. tall as Nancy 7. the youngest of

8. as, as the cat 9. earlier than 10. more than

■ Step 3 | Jump 1 p. 66

1. 비교급, 최상급, tall, faster, tallest, cute, larger,
cutest, hot, fatter, fattest, happy, happier,
easier, easiest, more, beautiful, most, popular
better, more, less, best, worst, least

2. 원급, 비교급

■ Step 3 | Jump 2 p. 67

1. larger 2. dark 3. harder 4. easiest

5. strongest 6. nicer 7. better 8. smartest

9. hot 10. newer 11. earlier 12. good

13. prettiest 14. in 15. fatter 16. more expensive

■ Step 3 | Jump 3   p. 68

1. lighter, than 2. newer, than 3. as, well, as
4. runs, faster 5. colder, than
6. the, most, important 7. higher, than
8. the, largest, city 9. less, than
10. more, interesting, than

■ Step 3 | Jump 4   p. 69

1. the most difficult subject.
2. play soccer better than baseball.
3. is as large as that room.
4. is the tallest student in his class.
5. live longer than men.
6. is shorter than Ann's hair.
7. is the biggest of the four.
8. is as old as my father.
9. This car is cheaper than that car.
10. This mountain is the highest in the world.

■ Step 4 | 실전 평가   p. 70

1. ④ 2. ① 3. ② 4. ③ 5. ④ 6. ③ 7. ② 8. ④
9. ① 10. lighter 11. higher, than 12. not, as, as
13. taller, than 14. ② 15. ① 16. ③ 17. well 18. of
19. tall as Julie 20. more expensive

1. 모음＋자음으로 끝나는 단어는 자음을 하나 더 써 주고
   -er, -est를 붙인다.
2. little의 최상급은 least이다.
3. pretty의 비교급과 최상급은 prettier, prettiest이다.
4. 문장에 than이 들어 있는 것으로 보아 들어갈 단어는
   비교급으로 expensive의 비교급은 more expensive
   이다.
5. '당신은 세상에서 가장 훌륭한 어머니이다'라는 뜻으로
   빈칸에는 최상급이 들어가야 한다.
6. as~as 원급을 이용한 비교급으로 빈칸에는 원급이 들
   어가야 한다.

7. ①, ③, ④번 문장은 비교급 문장으로 '~보다'라는 뜻
   의 than이 들어간다.
9. 첫 번째 문장은 비교급 문장이고 두 번째 문장은 최상
   급 문장이다.
13. Alex는 Mark보다 키다 크다.
14. ①은 비교급이 들어가야 하며 smart의 비교급은
   smarter이다. ④번은 최상급 문장으로 happiest가
   들어가야 한다.
15. fast의 비교급은 faster이고 cheap의 비교급은
   cheaper이다. ④번은 최상급 문장으로 tallest가 들
   어가야 한다.
16. healthy의 비교급은 healthier이고 thin의 비교급은
   thinner이다. ②번 문장은 원급 문장으로 sweet가 되
   어야 한다.

■ Step 5 | 서술형 평가   p. 72

A 1. worse, worst 2. warm, warmest
   3. more, most 4. famous, more famous
B 1. older 2. heavier 3. longer 4. shorter
C 1. as, as 2. taller, older 3. shortest

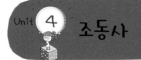

Unit 4 조동사

Pop Quiz

1. ❶ will ❷ ride

■ Step 1 | Check Up 1   p.77

1. ①, ③   **2.** ⑤, ⑥   **3.** ⑤, ⑦   **4.** ①, ④   **5.** ①, ②
6. ⑤, ⑥   **7.** ①, ②   **8.** ①, ③   **9.** ⑤, ⑦   **10.** ①, ③

■ Step 1 | Check Up 2   p.78

1. be   **2.** stays   **3.** start   **4.** ride   **5.** go   **6.** meets
7. study   **8.** speaks   **9.** go   **10.** do   **11.** eats
12. visit   **13.** be   **14.** helps   **15.** play   **16.** cleans

■ Step 1 | Check Up 3   p.79

1. pass   **2.** do   **3.** be   **4.** rescues   **5.** read
6. has to   **7.** eat   **8.** draw   **9.** have to   **10.** are
11. bring   **12.** chews   **13.** turn   **14.** have   **15.** be
16. rain

■ Step 1 | Check Up 4   p.80

1. My sister will leave this town.
2. He may buty the ticket.
3. The girl can play the piano in the hall.
4. The man is able to swim in the lake.
5. She has to exercise for her health.
6. Tom and Jane are able to meet in the park.
7. Her brother can make model planes.
8. Alice must go to see a doctor.
9. My parents will have lunch together.
10. My math textbook must be in school.

■ Step 1 | Check Up 5   p.81

1. My brother cannot[can't] fly the kite.
2. He must not write a letter to her.
3. Sophia may not come back home.
4. Brian is not[isn't] able to drive a car.
5. You must not throw away garbage.
6. Sarah may not be late again.
7. They don't have to meet him in the gallery.
8. She cannot[can't] cook the Italian food.

9. We are not[aren't] able to buy a present for him.
10. Jack doesn't have to wait for Peter.

■ Step 1 | Check Up 6   p.82

1. Can Julie use a computer?
2. Is my brother able to play the guitar?
3. Must people obey the law?
4. May I take a picture in the castle?
5. Are John and Tom able to go shopping with me?
6. May I ask you a question?
7. Must she take care of her brother?
8. Is your father able to play golf well?
9. Can you bring me the dictionary?
10. Are they able to bake a strawberry cake?

■ Step 2 | Build Up 1   p.83

1. You cannot[can't] borrow this book.
2. Can he play computer games now?
3. She doesn't have to wash the dishes.
4. We are not[aren't] able to live without water.
5. They must not finish the homework.
6. Can she go home now?
7. Is Peter able to speak French?
8. They may not help the sick girl.
9. The kid is not[isn't] able to read and write.
10. Can the boy remember his address?

■ Step 2 | Build Up 2   p.84

1. They cannot[can't] find the key in the room.
2. Judy must clean her room now.
3. Mr. Smith is able to help the poor child.
4. Is Ann able to come back home by eight?
5. May I draw your face there?
6. Is Tony able to fix his bike?
7. He doesn't have to visit my house on Sunday.
8. Jonathan must not run very fast.
9. Can you go on a picnic on Friday?
10. I will be able to play soccer in the park.

■ Step 2 | Build Up 3 — p.85

1. The boy cannot[can't] plant the flowers alone.,
   Can the boy plant the flowers alone?
2. Tom is not[isn't] able to walk to the park.,
   Is Tom able to walk to the park?
3. Yes, I can., No, I can't.
4. You must not leave my message.,
   You don't have to leave my message.
5. Yes, she is., No, she isn't.
6. We cannot[can't] play baseball at the playground., Can we play baseball at the playground?
7. They are not[aren't] able to buy the piano.,
   Are they able to buy the piano?

■ Step 3 | Jump 1 — p.86

1. 조동사, 할 수 있다, 임에 틀림없다, 일지도 모른다, able, to, have, to
2. 동사, 원형, play, play, able, not, Can, No
3. (1) can (2) has, to

■ Step 3 | Jump 2 — p.87

1. can 2. not 3. is 4. have 5. take
6. don't 7. be 8. be able to 9. rain
10. must 11. help 12. can't 13. has
14. must not 15. make 16. go

■ Step 3 | Jump 3 — p.88

1. James can use the chopsticks.
2. She has to repeat the word.
3. Are you able to help the sick people?
4. John will be able to teach history.
5. Peter and Mark must be very hungry.
6. Her brother can't[cannot] fix the chair.
7. He doesn't have to brush his teeth.
8. You are able to finish your homework.
9. It may rain this afternoon.

10. The kid is not[isn't] able to draw a nice picture.

■ Step 3 | Jump 4 — p.89

1. must[has to] hunt 2. don't have to go
3. may be sick 4. can[is able to] pass
5. cannot[can't] use 6. may not get
7. able to win 8. must not speak
9. able to buy 10. don't have to practice

■ Step 4 | 실전 평가 — p.90

1. ① 2. ③ 3. ③ 4. must 5. can 6. may 7. to
8. ② 9. ④ 10. ② 11. has to 12. don't have to do
13. ③ 14. ② 15. ① 16. ③ 17. doesn't have to
18. to take 19. must[have to] 20. don't have to

1. can은 be able to로 바꿀 수 있는데, 이때 be동사는 주어에 따라 맞게 쓴다.
2. must는 have to로 바꾸어 쓸 수 있다. 주어가 3인칭 단수일 경우에는 has to를 쓴다.
3. '나의 아버지는 바빠서 일찍 집에 올 수 없을 지도 모른다.'라는 뜻으로 추측에 해당하는 말이 와야 한다.
4. '~해야만 한다'라고 의무를 나타낼 때는 must를 쓴다.
5. '~할 수 있다'라고 가능을 나타낼 때는 can을 쓴다.
7. be able to는 '~할 수 있다'라는 뜻이고 have to는 '~해야만 한다'라는 뜻이다.
9. 조동사 다음에는 주어의 인칭에 상관없이 동사의 원형이 와야 한다. 또한 조동사는 2개를 연속으로 사용할 수 없다.
10. 조동사의 부정문은 조동사 다음에 not을 붙여서 만든다.
12. 불필요를 나타낼 때에는 don't have to를 사용하여 나타낸다.
13. ③번은 '~임에 틀림없다'라는 뜻으로 강한 추측을 나타낸다.
17. 주어가 3인칭 단수일 경우에는 doesn't have to로 쓴다.
18. be able to 다음에는 동사원형이 온다.

A **1.** are, able, to   **2.** has, to, see

B **1.** must not eat   **2.** must be   **3.** must not touch

C **1.** can, piano   **2.** can't, violin

Unit 5 동사의 과거시제

Pop Quiz

I. ❶ was ❷ was ❸ were

2. ❶ cried ❷ ran ❸ did

■ Step 1 | Check Up 1   p. 99

1. walked   **2.** hit   **3.** smiled   **4.** cut   **5.** stopped
6. brought   **7.** carried   **8.** had   **9.** looked
10. read   **11.** played   **12.** went   **13.** danced
14. came   **15.** planned   **16.** saw   **17.** liked
18. were   **19.** stayed   **20.** was   **21.** dropped
22. thought   **23.** worked   **24.** gave   **25.** opened
26. bought   **27.** listened   **28.** knew   **29.** visited
30. ate

■ Step 1 | Check Up 2   p. 100

1. worked   **2.** opened   **3.** smiled   **4.** stayed
5. listened   **6.** washed   **7.** enjoyed   **8.** planned
9. visited   **10.** dropped   **11.** played   **12.** walked
13. turned   **14.** tried   **15.** rained   **16.** loved

17. married   **18.** stopped   **19.** showed   **20.** passed
21. pushed   **22.** liked   **23.** carried   **24.** worried
25. studied   **26.** pulled   **27.** cried   **28.** danced
29. looked   **30.** lived

■ Step 1 | Check Up 3   p. 101

1. was   **2.** felt   **3.** let   **4.** understood   **5.** cost
6. shut   **7.** began   **8.** flew   **9.** bit   **10.** forgot
11. broke   **12.** forgave   **13.** meant   **14.** spoke
15. built   **16.** got   **17.** paid   **18.** stood   **19.** caught
20. went   **21.** quit   **22.** swam   **23.** came   **24.** hung
25. rode   **26.** taught   **27.** did   **28.** heard   **29.** drew
30. hid   **31.** ran   **32.** thought   **33.** drove   **34.** held
35. ate   **36.** hurt   **37.** sold   **38.** woke   **39.** fed
40. knew

■ Step 1 | Check Up 4   p. 102

1. lent   **2.** set   **3.** were   **4.** fought   **5.** became
6. found   **7.** wrote   **8.** sang   **9.** lost   **10.** sat
11. made   **12.** slept   **13.** brought   **14.** froze   **15.** met
16. spent   **17.** bought   **18.** gave   **19.** put   **20.** stole
21. chose   **22.** grew   **23.** read   **24.** took   **25.** cut
26. had   **27.** rang   **28.** won   **29.** rose   **30.** told
31. drank   **32.** hit   **33.** said   **34.** threw   **35.** saw
36. left   **37.** fell   **38.** kept   **39.** sent   **40.** wore

■ Step 1 | Check Up 5   p. 103

1. were   **2.** was   **3.** went   **4.** were   **5.** made
6. was   **7.** looked   **8.** were   **9.** gave   **10.** were
11. was   **12.** ate   **13.** were   **14.** stopped   **15.** were
16. played

■ Step 1 | Check Up 6   p. 104

1. bought   **2.** stayed   **3.** were   **4.** studied
5. fought   **6.** read   **7.** taught   **8.** made   **9.** drew
10. left   **11.** had   **12.** was   **13.** built   **14.** met
15. helped   **16.** found

■ Step 2 | Build Up 1   p. 105

1. Sam and John were kind police officers.

2. The young girl was very pretty.

3. Molly went to the subway with him.

4. She taught science at school.

5. Many students cleaned the street.

6. The school began at nine o'clock.

7. My father fixed the broken bike.

8. Julie caught a bad cold.

9. They stood in front of the gate.

10. Tony and Brian heard her voice.

■ Step 2 | Build Up 2   p. 106

1. wrote **2.** were **3.** started **4.** bought
5. thought **6.** knew **7.** visited **8.** finished
9. went **10.** ran **11.** sang **12.** met **13.** lost
14. came **15.** was **16.** left

■ Step 2 | Build Up 3   p. 107

1. drove **2.** moves **3.** became **4.** were **5.** is
6. invented **7.** went **8.** flows **9.** arrived **10.** rises
11. drew **12.** rode **13.** built **14.** stole **15.** drink
16. caught

■ Step 3 | Jump 1   p. 108

1. 과거형, yesterday, before, last, last, ago

2. was, were

3. ed, walked, played, d, liked, danced, cried, carried, 자음, stopped, planned, listened, opened

4. cut, thought, come, see, said, know, meet, gave

■ Step 3 | Jump 2   p. 109

1. was **2.** lost **3.** played **4.** lived **5.** took **6.** met
7. paid **8.** passed **9.** found **10.** were **11.** read

12. stayed **13.** saw **14.** finished **15.** became
16. collected

■ Step 3 | Jump 3   p. 110

1. Dorothy wore a hat last Sunday.

2. He dropped his pencil on the floor.

3. We had fun last weekend.

4. Adam wrote the novel in 1996.

5. John found the ring under the bed then.

6. Mark cut the rope with a knife.

7. Emily hurt her arm last Saturday.

8. Sophie heard the news two hours ago.

9. Sue told me the story two weeks ago.

10. The class ended at three p.m. yesterday.

■ Step 3 | Jump 4   p. 111

1. They went to the beach **2.** It was windy
3. I bought food **4.** She spoke English well
5. We won the game **6.** He went to the bed
7. James read the magazine **8.** Joe lost his dog
9. I sent a message **10.** Nick kept the promise

■ Step 4 | 실전 평가   p. 112

1. ② **2.** ④ **3.** ③ **4.** ④ **5.** ③ **6.** ② **7.** went **8.** ③
9. ② **10.** thought **11.** was
12. He lost his watch last month.
13. I saw a movie a few days ago. **14.** ③ **15.** ③
16. ② **17.** played tennis, swims **18.** boils, freezes
19. told **20.** lived

1. 동사의 규칙 변화 과거형은 단모음+단자음으로 끝나는 동사는 자음을 하나 더 쓰고 -ed를 붙인다. 또한 자음+y로 끝나는 동사는 y를 i로 바꾸고 -ed를 붙인다.

2. keep의 과거형은 불규칙 변화로 kept이다.

3. swim의 과거형은 swam이다.

4. 문장의 끝에 ago가 있으므로 과거 문장이 와야 한다.

5. 문장에 last month가 있는 것으로 보아 과거 문장으로 빈칸에 들어갈 말은 동사의 과거형이 와야 한다.

6. 문장의 동사에 meet의 과거형인 met이 온 것으로 보아 과거를 나타내는 말이 와야 한다.

7. go의 과거형은 불규칙 변화로 went이다.

9. eat의 과거형은 ate이다.

12. lose의 과거형은 lost이고 지난달은 last month이다.

13. see의 과거형은 saw이고 며칠 전은 a few days ago이다.

14. she and he는 복수형으로 was가 아닌 were가 되어야 한다.

15. 과거를 나타내는 last weekend가 있으므로 cook을 과거형인 cooked로 써야 한다.

16. ②번은 과거 문장으로 동사도 과거형인 had로 써야 한다.

18. 일반적인 사실이나 현상을 나타내므로 현재형으로 나타내야 한다.

■ **Step 5 ┃ 서술형 평가**   p. 114

A Yesterday was a very exciting day for me. My classmates went on a trip to the fire station. We went to the fire station by bus, but it rained. We ate lunch inside the fire station with all the fire fighters. They were nice and funny. We got on the fire truck and rang the bell on the truck. And we walked around the fire station. I saw a dog. The dog was a dalmatian. It was black and white. It was a great fun day!

B **1.** had short, has long **2.** went to, goes to

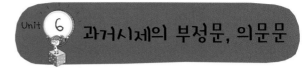

Unit 6 과거시제의 부정문, 의문문

Pop Quiz

1. ❶ was ❷ were
2. ❶ did ❷ Did

■ **Step 1 ┃ Check Up 1**   p. 119

1. didn't, carry **2.** Did, spend **3.** were, not
4. didn't, find **5.** Did, stop **6.** didn't, drive
7. Did, sell **8.** was, not **9.** Did, need
10. Did, meet

■ **Step 1 ┃ Check Up 2**   p. 120

1. didn't, play **2.** didn't, catch **3.** Did, see
4. Was, hungry **5.** didn't, give **6.** Did, believe
7. Were, late **8.** didn't, build **9.** Did, write
10. didn't, understand

■ **Step 1 ┃ Check Up 3**   p. 121

1. Amy and Alice were not[weren't] young then.
2. The Jacket was not[wasn't] expensive.
3. He was not[wasn't] interested in soccer.
4. We were not[weren't] tired and thirsty.
5. It was not[wasn't] hot the day before yesterday.
6. My father was not[wasn't] a fire fighter.
7. Susan was not[wasn't] afraid of dogs.
8. Your sneakers were not[weren't] very dirty.
9. Jenny was not[wasn't] in the classroom then.
10. The tomatoes were not[weren't] in the bowl.

■ **Step 1 ┃ Check Up 4**   p. 122

1. He did not[didn't] make the bench a week ago.
2. She did not[didn't] eat two pieces of cake.
3. She did not[didn't] finish the work yesterday.

4. Mark did not[didn't] know the way to the gallery.

5. They did not[didn't] buy vegetables then.

6. She did not[didn't] enjoy the party last night.

7. He did not[didn't] have a nice car last year.

8. Matt did not[didn't] read a newspaper yesterday.

9. We did not[didn't] play the piano well.

10. My family did not[didn't] go fishing last week.

■ **Step 1** | **Check Up 5** p. 123

1. Did she live in New York two years ago?

2. Were you late for the meeting yesterday?

3. Did the people have a nice winter vacation?

4. Was the window broken then?

5. Did his brother call you last week?

6. Did Nick leave here three months ago?

7. Did Susie plant the flowers in the garden?

8. Was it cold in Canada at that time?

9. Did Tom and Ann see a movie at the theater?

10. Were your mom and dad in England?

■ **Step 1** | **Check Up 6** p. 124

1. he was, he wasn't 2. I did, I didn't

3. they were, they weren't

4. she was, she wasn't

5. they did, they didn't

6. she did, she didn't

7. they did, they didn't

8. he did, he didn't

9. they were, they weren't

10. she did, she didn't

■ **Step 2** | **Build Up 1** p. 125

1. Kevin did not[didn't] talk with the friends.

2. Did he break the window yesterday?

3. Thomas did not[didn't] kick the ball in the park.

4. Did my sister write the diary last night?

5. Did the student ask some questions?

6. They did not[didn't] drink milk in the morning.

7. My father did not[didn't] teach math at school.

8. Did the boy carry the heavy box?

9. Did she listen to music last night?

10. The girl did not[didn't] swim with the mother.

■ **Step 2** | **Build Up 2** p. 126

1. Did Eric ride a horse two hours ago?

2. Did the visitor see beautiful towers there?

3. The men did not[didn't] climb up the mountain.

4. Did the baby sleep on the bed then?

5. It rained a few days ago.

6. The spider did not[didn't] come down the tree.

7. Did Sally have a great summer vacation?

8. Did they clean the classroom yesterday?

9. He did not[didn't] receive an e-mail from her.

10. My brother did not[didn't] speak Chinese well.

■ **Step 2** | **Build Up 3** p. 127

1. Kate did not[didn't] make the same mistake.

2. She did not[didn't] put her ring here yesterday.

3. Did the kid remember you at that time?

4. Did Huck paint the wall last month?

5. The drivers were not[weren't] busy and tired.

6. Ashley did not[didn't] buy a new sweater.

7. Was her cousin young and pretty?

8. Did Joe pass the exam last week?

9. Were they thirteen years old last year?

10. The judge did not[didn't] punish the bad man.

■ **Step 3** | **Jump 1** p. 128

1. am, are, is, not, wasn't, weren't

2. Was, Were, Was 3. didn't, do, does, didn't

4. Did, Does, Did

■ Step 3 I Jump 2   p. 129

1. Was Tom at the market?, he wasn't
2. Did Mark solve the riddle?, he did
3. Were they so happy then?, they were
4. Did the man catch a bear?, he didn't
5. Did she read the novel yesterday?, she did
6. Was her father a pilot?, he was
7. Did the bats live in this cave?, they didn't
8. Did it rain last Sunday?, it did
9. Were the shoes cheap?, they weren't
10. Did they win the game last month?, they did

■ Step 3 I Jump 3   p. 130

1. made, make   2. Was, Were   3. looked, look
4. got, get   5. Do, Did   6. not, didn't
7. sleeps, sleep   8. called, call   9. lose, lost
10. do, did   11. Were, Was   12. didn't, wasn't
13. was, were   14. smiles, smile   15. spent, spend
16. left, leave

■ Step 3 I Jump 4   p. 131

1. meet, go, run / met, went, ran
2. No – she didn't   3. Yes – they did
4. No – they didn't   5. No – they didn't
6. Yes – she did

■ Step 4 I 실전 평가   p. 132

1. ④ 2. ② 3. ③ 4. ② 5. ① 6. ③ 7. Was, wasn't
8. ③ 9. ③ 10. ① 11. ③ 12. ④ 13. was, not
14. ② 15. was, were 16. went, go 17. ③ 18. ②
19. ② 20. ③

1. he and she로 보아 복수 주어로 are나 were가 들어
   갈 수 있는데, 문장에 과거를 나타내는 then이 있는 것
   으로 보아 과거 문장이라는 것을 알 수 있다.
2. yesterday가 문장에 있는 것으로 보아 be동사의 과거

형이 들어가야 한다.
3. soldiers는 복수형으로 was가 아닌 were와 함께 써
   야 한다.
4. last year가 문장에 있는 것으로 보아 과거형 문장으
   로 동사의 경우 went를 써야 한다.
5. at that time이라는 과거를 나타내는 문구가 있는 것으
   로 보아 과거형 문장으로 didn't를 써야 한다.
6. 첫 번째 문장은 과거형 문장으로 동사의 과거형이 와
   야 하고 두 번째 문장은 현재형 문장으로 동사의 현재
   형이 와야 한다.
9. 명사의 단수형은 were가 아닌 was와 함께 쓴다.
10. 과거형 문장의 의문문은 Did 다음에 주어가 오고 그
    뒤에 동사는 동사원형으로 써 준다.
11. 과거형 문장의 부정문은 동사 앞에 did not(= didn't)
    를 쓰고 동사는 동사원형으로 써 준다.
14. were not의 축약형은 weren't이다.
17. 과거형 문장의 대답은 Yes나 No를 사용하여 하는데,
    일반동사 의문문은 did를 이용하여 답한다.
18. be동사의 과거형 의문문은 was나 were를 이용하여
    답한다.

■ Step 5 I 서술형 평가   p. 134

A 1. liked, didn't, like   2. didn't, leave, left
B 1. 예) I visited my grandparents last weekend. /
     I ate spaghetti at the restaurant yesterday.
     / I swam in the swimming pool a few days
     ago.
   2. 예) I didn't visit my grandparents last weekend.
     / I didn't eat spaghetti at the restaurant
     yesterday. / I didn't swim in the swimming
     pool a few days ago.

Unit 7 과거진행형

Pop Quiz

1. ❶ coming ❷ studying ❸ running
2. ❶ was ❷ were

■ Step 1 ı Check Up 1   p. 139

1. jumping 2. carrying 3. coming 4. building
5. playing 6. reading 7. running 8. taking
9. writing 10. seeing 11. riding 12. lying
13. sleeping 14. climbing 15. sending 16. feeling
17. studying 18. planning 19. making 20. falling
21. walking 22. buying 23. dying 24. saying
25. cooking 26. bringing 27. listening 28. cutting
29. eating 30. dancing

■ Step 1 ı Check Up 2   p. 140

1. snowing 2. was 3. were 4. had
5. helping 6. were 7. belonged
8. flying 9. playing 10. writing 11. was
12. were 13. were 14. remembered
15. swimming 16. were

■ Step 1 ı Check Up 3   p. 141

1. was playing 2. were sitting 3. were making
4. was watching 5. was doing 6. were going
7. were sleeping 8. was listening 9. was cleaning
10. were visiting 11. was buying 12. were skiing
13. were having 14. was driving 15. was walking
16. were solving

■ Step 1 ı Check Up 4   p. 142

1. was sitting 2. were running 3. was walking
4. was singing 5. was playing 6. was riding

7. were drawing 8. were playing 9. was flying
10. were having

■ Step 2 ı Build Up 1   p. 143

1. My father was driving to the market.
2. Amy was reading the guidebook.
3. The people were bringing a lot of silver.
4. The students were solving the easy problem.
5. The rain was falling heavily from the sky.
6. We were catching the dragonfly.
7. The kangaroo was jumping high.
8. The soccer player was kicking the ball.
9. It was snowing a lot in New York.
10. They were eating some bread for lunch.

■ Step 2 ı Build Up 2   p. 144

1. Nick was not[wasn't] exercising at the gym.
2. They were not[weren't] lying to their parents.
3. The men were not[weren't] staying at the hotel.
4. Judy was not[wasn't] drinking lemonade.
5. You were not[weren't] digging a big hole.
6. I was not[wasn't] reading a novel at that time.
7. We were not[weren't] standing in front of the door.
8. Cathy was not[wasn't] studying two languages.
9. The children were not[weren't] having lunch.
10. He was not[wasn't] using the Internet.

■ Step 2 ı Build Up 3   p. 145

1. Was the dog barking at him? / it was.
2. Were they building a castle? / they weren't.
3. Were birds flying to the south? / they were.
4. Were you doing your best? / I was[we were].
5. Was Tom taking a shower? / he wasn't.
6. Was Sally cutting the cake? / she was.
7. Was Kevin riding a bicycle? / he wasn't.
8. Were Dan and Ann selling donuts? / they were.

9. Was she sleeping on the sofa? / she wasn't.

10. Was Dorothy singing a song? / she was.

Step 3 | Jump 1
p. 146

1. 진행, 과거, am, are, is, 과거, were
2. belong, hate, know, remember
3. was, were, not, not, ing
4. 주어, be, be, 주어, Yes, No

Step 3 | Jump 2
p. 147

1. They were talking with their teacher.
2. The player was not[wasn't] kicking the ball.
3. I was not[wasn't] touching the china.
4. Was he cooking in the kitchen?
5. Peter was laughing at me.
6. Was Joseph sending a text message?
7. We were not[weren't] waiting for Susie.
8. He was not[wasn't] listening to the radio.
9. My son was putting forks on the table.
10. Was his mother buying many things?

Step 3 | Jump 3
p. 148

1. was watching 2. were flying 3. was playing
4. were swimming 5. were carrying
6. was singing 7. were having 8. was helping
9. was writing 10. was coming 11. were studying
12. was hugging

Step 3 | Jump 4
p. 149

1. were, was 2. wasn't, weren't 3. takeing, taking
4. was knowing, knew 5. did, was
6. not was, was not 7. were having, had
8. weren't, wasn't 9. Was, Were
10. cookking, cooking 11. was, were
12. is resembling, resembles 13. weren't, wasn't
14. Was, Were 15. were, was
16. was remembering, remembered

Step 4 | 실전 평가
p. 150

1. ③ 2. ② 3. ④ 4. ② 5. ③ 6. were, walking
7. was, wearing 8. ① 9. ③ 10. ② 11. ③ 12. ③
13. ④ 14. ④ 15. ①
16. They were not jogging after lunch.
17. My cat was not[wasn't] sleeping on the sofa.
18. Was her son brushing his teeth?
19. was having lunch
20. were doing their homework

1. -e로 끝나는 동사는 e를 삭제하고 -ing를 붙인다.
2. -ie로 끝나는 동사는 ie를 y로 바꾸고 -ing를 붙인다.
4. resemble(닮다)은 진행형으로 쓸 수 없는 동사이다.
5. 과거진행형 문장은 was/were 다음에 동사의 -ing로 쓴다.
7. 주어가 1인칭, 3인칭 단수일 때는 was를 쓴다.
8. 과거진행형 의문문은 Yes나 No를 사용하여 답한다.
9. 주어가 명사일 경우에 여자이면 she로, 남자이면 he로 답한다.
10. Tom and Ann은 복수 명사로 were를 써야 한다.
11. 여기서 have는 '소유하다'라는 뜻으로 진행형을 쓸 수 없다.
13. 과거진행형은 be동사+동사의 -ing형으로 쓴다.
14. 단수 명사는 was를 사용하여 나타낸다.
15. Jim and I는 복수 명사로 were를 사용하여 나타낸다.
17. 과거진행형 부정문은 be동사의 부정문 만드는 방법과 같은데, be동사 뒤에 not을 붙여서 만든다.

Step 5 | 서술형 평가
p. 152

A 1. was, riding 2. is, playing
B 1. was, doing 2. was, watching, TV
   3. was, having, dinner 4. is, taking

Unit 8 동사의 미래시제

Pop Quiz

1. ❶ be ❷ go
2. meet

■ Step 1 ㅣ Check Up 1   p. 157

1. listen 2. will 3. is 4. will, play 5. hunt
6. be 7. take 8. is, wash 9. will
10. will, invite 11. be 12. meet 13. will
14. is, buy 15. are 16. fly

■ Step 1 ㅣ Check Up 2   p. 158

1. is going to arrive 2. will send
3. are going to help 4. am going to start
5. will have 6. is going to land
7. will move 8. will travel
9. is going to order
10. am going to play

■ Step 1 ㅣ Check Up 3   p. 159

1. will be 2. will make 3. are going to buy
4. will visit 5. will leave 6. is going to attend
7. are going to learn 8. will write
9. will be 10. is going to do
11. are going to see 12. will dance
13. will build 14. will take
15. will eat 16. is going to sell

■ Step 1 ㅣ Check Up 4   p. 160

1. will drive 2. will take 3. are going to turn
4. will wash 5. are going to drink
6. am going to walk 7. will come
8. will be 9. are going to live 10. will study

11. will be 12. is going to stay 13. will cut
14. is going to call 15. will swim 16. will fix

■ Step 1 ㅣ Check Up 5   p. 161

1. It will not[won't] be fine tomorrow.
2. We are not[aren't] going to get there by subway.
3. He is not[isn't] going to use much water.
4. Kate and Ann will not[won't] have oranges.
5. I will not[won't] be twelve years old next year.
6. She is not[isn't] going to paint the house soon.
7. They will not[won't] be surprised at the news.
8. I am not going to watch a movie tonight.
9. Sam is not[isn't] going to go to the concert.
10. Jess will not[won't] bring some wine next week.

■ Step 1 ㅣ Check Up 6   p. 162

1. Is the class going to end in ten minutes?
2. Will Kate and Jill like the presents?
3. Will she tell him about the truth?
4. Is Lisa going to be angry at her sister?
5. Will Joe help you with your homework?
6. Will Tom's father give him a chance?
7. Is John going to have a party?
8. Will he visit his uncle next month?
9. Are Bob and Tom going to stay at the hotel?
10. Will she buy a new chair next weekend?

■ Step 2 ㅣ Build Up 1   p. 163

1. He is going to cook dinner for you.
2. They are going to stay in Jeju for a week.
3. She is going to follow the rules.
4. Alex is going to join the club.
5. I am going to finish the work soon.
6. Sally is going to be in her room.
7. My mother is going to visit my aunt soon.

8. I am going to meet her in the department store.

9. Sam is going to build the sand castle there.

10. You are going to save money for his birthday.

■ Step 2 ı Build Up 2   p.164

1. She will bring you the ball.

2. I am going to take a trip.

3. Tom and his sister will draw pictures.

4. The woman will make some cookies.

5. He is going to take off his coat.

6. We are going to bake some bread.

7. My mother will clean up my room.

8. He will wait for you in front of the bank.

9. I am going to read books in my room.

10. Jenny is going to do her homework.

■ Step 2 ı Build Up 3   p.165

1. We will go to see a movie tomorrow.

2. My brother will be a high school student next month.

3. I will be able to travel around the world some day.

4. She will buy an expensive car next week.

5. His father will come back home soon.

6. The woman will leave this country next year.

7. Ann and Eric will move to Paris tomorrow.

8. Sally and Lisa will meet at the bookstore next time.

9. They will go on a picnic to the river next week.

10. We will be able to see the star clearly tomorrow.

■ Step 3 ı Jump 1   p.166

1. will, be going to, will, be going to, 동사원형

2. day, after, week, next, soon

3. I'll, You'll, He'll, She'll, It'll, We'll, They'll

4. not, will 5. 주어, not, 주어

6. 왕래발착, 현재

■ Step 3 ı Jump 2   p.167

1. He will be a famous musician.

2. Sally is not[isn't] going to wear a pink dress.

3. She will not[won't] walk to the station.

4. Eric is going to exercise at the gym.

5. Jane will not[won't] make sandwiches.

6. My father is not[isn't] going to fix the door.

7. We will remember Sue's address.

8. Tommy is going to pass the exam.

9. It will not[won't] rain a lot.

10. My mother is not[isn't] going to close the window.

■ Step 3 ı Jump 3   p.168

1. Will they lend their houses?, they will.

2. Is he going to have a job?, he is.

3. Will the cat live in your house?, it won't.

4. Will she disappear after the show?, she will.

5. Is Kate going to came back soon?, she isn't.

6. Will Tony and Judy study hard?, they will.

7. Is he going to enjoy his life?, he isn't.

8. Are they going to play soccer?, they are.

9. Will the train arrive in ten minutes?, it won't.

10. Will Tom and Jane go there?, they will.

■ Step 3 ı Jump 4   p.169

1. helps → help 2. played → play

3. stays → stay 4. are → is 5. going → go

6. moving → move 7. walks → walk 8. of → to

9. lends → lend 10. drinks → drink

11. are going not → are not going

12. wills → will 13. is going to → will

14. are → is 15. rides → ride

16. kicking → kick

1. ② 2. ② 3. ④ 4. ③ 5. ③ 6. ② 7. ① 8. ①
9. ③ 10. ④ 11. ③ 12. ② 13. ① 14. ③ 15. ①
16. rained, raining, rains, rain
17. came, His father will come back home soon.
18. passing, Tommy is going to pass the exam.
19. is going to exercise   20. won't buy

1. be going to가 있는 문장의 부정문은 be동사 뒤에 not을 붙여서 만든다.

2. 조동사 will이 있는 문장의 부정문은 will 뒤에 not을 붙이면 된다.

3. 문장에 in ten minutes라는 문구가 있는 것으로 보아 미래형 문장이라는 것을 알 수 있다.

4. last night, ago, yesterday는 과거를 나타내는 말들이다.

5. 조동사 will 뒤에는 항상 동사원형이 온다.

6. 조동사 will의 부정문은 will 뒤에 not을 붙여서 만들며 will not의 축약형은 won't이다.

7. 질문의 대답에 won't가 있는 것으로 보아 미래형 문장이라는 것을 알 수 있다. 따라서 will이나 be going to 의문문을 찾으면 된다.

8. will로 물어보면 Yes, No를 이용하여 will로 답한다.

11. be going to를 이용한 미래형 문장에서 be동사는 현재시제(am, are, is)를 사용한다.

12. won't(= will not) 뒤에는 항상 동사원형이 온다.

15. 왕래발착(가다, 오다, 출발하다, 도착하다) 동사는 현재시제로 정해지고 계획된 미래의 일을 나타낼 수 있다.

16. 지난 일은 과거형으로, 현재의 사실은 현재형으로, 진행되고 있는 것은 진행형으로 나타내며 앞으로의 일은 미래형으로 나타낸다.

A 1. No, he won't.   2. Yes, he will.   3. Yes, she is.
B 1. is swimming   2. is going to watch

1. ③ 2. ① 3. ④ 4. ① 5. ② 6. ③ 7. ④ 8. ③
9. ② 10. ② 11. ③ 12. ④ 13. ③ 14. ① 15. ③
16. ④ 17. ② 18. ③ 19. ① 20. ②

1. famous의 비교급과 최상급은 more와 most를 붙여서 만든다.

2. short에 -er이 붙어 비교급으로 쓰인 것으로 보아 비교 문장으로 '~ 보다'에 해당하는 than이 와야 한다.

3. 최상급 문장에서 his class라고 비교 범위가 나온 것으로 보아 전치사 in이 와야 한다.

4. 앞에 나온 명사와 같은 종류이지만 불특정한 것을 나타낼 때는 one을 쓴다.

5. Sally가 Judy보다 어리다는 것은 즉, Judy가 Sally보다 나이가 많다는 것이다.

6. they의 재귀대명사는 themselves이다.

7. all은 대명사와 형용사로 쓰이는데 사람이면 복수, 사물이면 단수 취급한다.

8. 미래의 의미를 나타낼 때는 will 또는 be going to로 나타낸다. be going to에서 be동사는 주어에 따라 맞게 쓴다.

9. must는 의무와 강한 추측으로 쓰이는데 의무로 쓰일 때는 have to로 쓸 수 있다. 주어가 3인칭 단수일 때에는 has to로 쓴다.

12. can으로 물어보는 의문문은 Yes나 No를 사용하여 답한다. 대답이 부정일 때는 can't를 사용한다.

13. 과거진행형 문장은 주어+be동사(was, were)+동사의 -ing형으로 쓴다. 의문문의 경우에는 be동사+주어+동사의 -ing형 ~?로 나타낸다.

14. 바다에서 수영을 할 수 있다는 가능의 조동사 can이 와야 한다.

15. 내년에는 12살이 될 것이라는 미래를 나타내는 조동사 will이 와야 한다.

17. 문장에 ago가 있는 것으로 보아 과거형 문장으로 빈칸에는 동사의 과거형이 와야 한다.

1. ④ 2. ① 3. ③ 4. is able to 5. ③ 6. ② 7. ④
8. ① 9. ④ 10. ① 11. ③ 12. ② 13. ④ 14. ③
15. ② 16. met 17. He didn't see her there.
18. ② 19. ① 20. ④

1. second, twelfth, hundredth는 순서를 나타내는 서수
이다.

2. 3의 기수는 three이고 서수는 third이다.

3. best는 good의 최상급으로 두 단어의 관계는 원급과
최상급을 나타낸다.

4. can이 가능으로 쓰일 때는 be able to로 바꾸어 쓸
수 있다.

5. 그녀 칼로 베었다는 뜻으로 재귀대명사가 와야 한다.
she의 재귀대명사는 herself이다.

6. interesting의 비교급은 more interesting이다.

7. both는 대명사와 형용사로 쓰이는데 복수 취급한다.

8. 동사에 has가 쓰인 것으로 보아 단수 취급을 하는 대
명사를 찾아야 한다. every의 경우에는 그 뒤에 단수
명사가 바로 온다.

11. tomorrow, next Sunday, soon은 미래를 나타내는
말들이다.

12. 추측과 허가의 의미로 쓰이는 조동사는 may이다.

13. 강한 추측과 의무의 의미로 쓰이는 조동사는 must이
다.

14. 조동사 2개를 동시에 연속으로 사용할 수 없으므로
can을 be able to로 바꾸어 will과 함께 쓰면 된다.

15. think의 과거형은 thought이다.

16. last weekend라는 과거를 나타내는 말이 있으므로
과거형 동사가 와야 한다.

20. 과거진행형 부정문은 주어+was/were+not+동사
의 -ing형으로 나타낸다.

초등 영어 교재의 베스트셀러

초등 영어 문법 실력 쌓기!

Grammar Builder 3

Grammar Builder 시리즈

Words in Grammar

UK

You Are the Only One!

I am books

Grammar
Builder
시리즈

초등 영어 교재의 베스트셀러

초등 영어 문법 실력 쌓기!

Grammar Builder 3

You Are the Only One!

Words in Grammar

iam books

collect	모으다	She collects ten coins.	그녀는 동전 10개를 모은다.
bus stop	버스 정류장	Here is the third bus stop from my house.	여기는 나의 집에서 3번째 버스 정류장이다.
line	선	The boy is the sixth in this line.	그 소년은 이 줄에서 6번째이다.
floor	층, 마루	The hospital is on the third floor.	그 병원은 3층에 있다.
send	보내다	Tom sends nine e-mails to her.	Tom은 그녀에게 이메일 9통을 보낸다.
grade	학년, 등급	My brother is in the first grade.	나의 남동생은 1학년이다.
basket	바구니	There is one apple in the basket.	바구니에 사과가 1개 있다.
postcard	엽서	Max sends nine postcards to the friends.	Max는 친구들에게 엽서 9장을 보낸다.
meal	식사	This is his third meal today.	이것은 오늘 그의 3번째 식사이다.
finger	손가락	We have ten fingers.	우리는 10개의 손가락이 있다.
minute	분	It takes thirty minutes to get there.	거기에 도착하는데 30분이 걸린다.
Arbor Day	식목일	We plant fifty trees on Arbor Day.	우리는 식목일에 나무 50그루를 심는다.
story	층	This is a building of sixty-three stories.	이것은 63층 건물이다.
button	버튼, 단추	Please push the second button.	2번째 버튼을 누르세요.
block	블록, 구역	Go straight four blocks.	곧장 4블록 가세요.
left	왼쪽	It is the fifth building on your left.	그것은 너의 왼쪽에서 5번째 건물이다.
symphony	심포니	This music is his sixth Symphony.	이 음악은 그의 6번째 심포니이다.
anniversary	기념일	Today is our thirtieth wedding anniversary.	오늘은 우리의 결혼 30주년이다.
novel	소설	It is Jennifer's eighth novel.	그것은 Jennifer의 8번째 소설이다.
playground	운동장	There are thirty people on the playground.	운동장에 30명이 있다.
difficult	어려운	The third question is very difficult.	3번째 문제는 매우 어렵다.
gallery	미술관	Here is the fourth station from the gallery.	여기는 미술관으로부터 4번째 역이다.
bank	은행	The bank is the seventh building.	그 은행은 7번째 건물이다.
letter	편지	Judy sends ten letters to her friends.	Judy는 그녀의 친구들에게 편지 10통을 보낸다.
medicine	약	Take this medicine thirty minutes after a meal.	이 약을 식사 후 30분에 드세요.
trip	여행	This is my second trip to Japan.	이번이 나의 2번째 일본 여행이다.
tomorrow	내일	Tomorrow is the first day of the middle school.	내일이 중학교에서의 첫 날이다.
birthday	생일	My birthday is on October thirty-first.	나의 생일은 10월 31일이다.
different	다른	There are two different endings of the story.	그 이야기는 2가지의 다른 결말이 있다.
number	번호	His phone number is one two three four five six seven.	그의 전화번호는 123-4567번이다.

lend	빌려주다	Please lend me an eraser.	제발 지우개를 빌려주세요.
own	자신의	Each of the boys has his own room.	그 소년들 각각 자신의 방을 가지고 있다.
talent	재주, 재능	Both of them have a talent for art.	그들 둘 다 미술에 재능이 있다.
greedy	욕심 많은	Every man is greedy.	모든 남자는 욕심이 많다.
diligent	근면한	All of them are very diligent.	그들 모두 매우 근면하다.
useful	유용한	Some of the books are very useful.	그 책들의 몇몇은 매우 유용하다.
furniture	가구	Some of the furniture is expensive.	그 가구의 일부는 비싸다.
different	다른	Each of them is from a different country.	그들 각각 다른 나라 출신이다.
fault	잘못	It is not your fault.	그것은 너의 잘못이 아니다.
proud	자랑스러운	The boys are proud of themselves.	그 소년들은 스스로 자랑스러워한다.
borrow	빌리다	Can I borrow a ruler?	내가 자를 빌려도 될까요?
hide	숨기다	The kids hide themselves under the table.	그 소년들은 탁자 밑에 그들 자신을 숨긴다.
blond	금발의	Every girl has short blond hair.	모든 소녀는 짧은 금발 머리이다.
only	단지	He only thinks about himself.	그는 단지 그 자신만을 생각한다.
ask	질문하다	Another student asks the question.	다른 학생이 그 문제를 질문한다.
among	~의 사이에	Among them, I like the green one.	그것들 사이에서 초록색의 것을 좋아한다.
empty	빈	All of these seat are empty.	이 자리의 모두가 비워 있다.
prepare	준비하다	All girls prepare for the exam.	모든 소녀들은 시험을 위해 준비한다.
silent	조용한	Both of them are silent.	그들 둘 다 조용하다.
information	정보	Some of the information is useful.	그 정보의 일부는 유용하다.
introduce	소개하다	I introduce myself to my new neighbor.	나는 새 이웃에게 나를 소개한다.
ride	타다	The girl rides the bike herself.	그 소녀는 스스로 자전거를 탄다.
believe	믿다	You need to believe in yourselves.	너희들은 너희를 믿는 게 필요하다.
outgoing	사교적인	Every girl in the class is outgoing.	그 반의 모든 소녀는 사교적이다.
thick	두꺼운	Both of his books are very thick.	그의 책 둘 다 매우 두껍다.
drop	떨어지다	Some of the water is dropping.	그 물의 일부가 떨어지고 있다.
protect	보호하다	We must protect ourselves from the enemies.	우리는 적으로부터 우리 자신을 보호해야 한다.
travel	여행하다	We travel some countries in Europe.	우리는 유럽의 몇몇 나라를 여행한다.

early	일찍	I get up earlier than my sister.	나는 나의 여동생보다 일찍 일어난다.
brave	용감한	He is the bravest man in our town.	그는 우리 마을에서 가장 용감한 남자이다.
subject	과목	The most difficult subject is math.	가장 어려운 과목은 수학이다.
island	섬	Jeju island is the largest island in Korea.	제주도는 한국에서 가장 큰 섬이다.
steel	강철	The steel is harder than the stone.	그 강철은 그 돌보다 단단하다.
place	장소	Here is the most dangerous place in the town.	여기는 마을에서 가장 위험한 곳이다.
mountain	산	Mt. Baekdu is the highest mountain in Korea.	백두산은 한국에서 가장 높은 산이다.
artist	화가	He is the most famous artist in the world.	그는 세계에서 가장 유명한 화가이다.
boring	지루한	This book is more boring than the movie.	이 책은 그 영화보다 더 지루하다.
sweet	달콤한	The apple is not as sweet as this orange.	그 사과는 이 오렌지만큼 달지 않다.
today	오늘	Today is colder than yesterday.	오늘은 어제보다 더 춥다.
quick	빠른	Thomas is as quick as a cat.	Thomas는 고양이만큼 빠르다.
thing	물건, 것	The worst thing is the war.	가장 나쁜 것은 전쟁이다.
weigh	무게가 나가다	The cat weighs 5kg.	그 고양이는 5kg이 나간다.
rain	비가 오다	It rained 15mm in Seoul.	서울에는 15mm의 비가 내렸다.
dark	어두운	This place is as dark as that place.	이곳은 저곳만큼 어둡다.
wood	목재	The steel is harder than the wood.	그 강철은 그 목재보다 단단하다.
smart	영리한	Tom is the smartest boy in this city.	Tom은 이 도시에서 가장 영리한 소년이다.
fat	뚱뚱한	That girl is fat than this boy.	저 소녀는 이 소년보다 더 뚱뚱하다.
cook	요리하다	Mr. Smith cooks better than his wife.	Smith 씨는 그의 부인보다 요리를 더 잘한다.
husband	남편	She cooks as well as her husband.	그녀는 그녀의 남편만큼 요리를 잘한다.
important	중요한	This is the most important work.	이것은 가장 중요한 업무이다.
animation	만화영화	That is more interesting than the animation.	저것은 만화영화보다 더 재미있다.
baseball	야구	They play soccer better than baseball.	그들은 야구보다 축구를 더 잘한다.
live	살다	Women live longer than men.	여자는 남자보다 더 오래 산다.
hair	머리카락	My hair is shorter than Ann's hair.	나의 머리카락은 Ann의 머리카락보다 더 짧다.
cheap	싼	This car is cheaper than that car.	이 차는 저 차보다 더 싸다.
busy	바쁜	She is the busiest of the five.	그녀는 다섯 중에 가장 바쁘다.
popular	인기 있는	He is as popular as an actor.	그는 배우만큼 인기가 많다.
cute	귀여운	Your puppy is the cutest of the four.	너의 강아지는 그 넷 중에 가장 귀엽다.

rule	규칙	We must follow the rules.	우리는 그 규칙을 따라야만 한다.
exercise	운동하다	Peter has to exercise every day.	Peter는 매일 운동해야만 한다.
understand	이해하다	I can understand this thick book.	나는 이 두꺼운 책을 이해할 수 있다.
alone	홀로	I can move this box alone.	나는 홀로 이 상자를 운반할 수 있다.
stay	머무르다	She stays in her room.	그녀는 그녀의 방에 머무른다.
station	역	Julia meets John at the station.	Julia는 그 역에서 John을 만난다.
tonight	오늘밤	He may go to the party tonight.	그는 오늘밤에 그 파티에 갈지도 모른다.
clean	청소하다	She cleans her room every day.	그녀는 매일 그녀의 방을 청소한다.
rescue	구조하다	The police officer rescues the child.	그 경찰관이 그 어린이를 구조한다.
weekend	주말	We can swim this weekend.	우리는 이번 주말에 수영할 수 있다.
chew	씹다	Ashley chews the gum.	Ashley는 그 껌을 씹는다.
ticket	표	He gives her the ticket.	그는 그녀에게 그 표를 준다.
health	건강	She exercises for her health.	그녀는 그녀의 건강을 위해 운동한다.
model	모형	Her brother makes model planes.	그녀의 남동생은 모형 비행기를 만든다.
textbook	교과서	My math textbook is in school.	나의 수학 교과서는 학교에 있다.
garbage	쓰레기	You must not throw away garbage.	너는 쓰레기를 버려서는 안 된다.
obey	복종하다	People obey the law.	사람들은 법을 복종한다.
castle	성	I take a picture in the castle.	나는 성에서 사진을 찍는다.
address	주소	Can the boy remember his address?	그 소년은 그의 주소를 기억할 수 있니?
plant	심다	The boy can plant the flowers.	그 소년은 꽃들을 심을 수 있다.
message	메시지	You must leave my message.	너는 나의 메시지를 받아야 한다.
receive	받다	Is she able to receive the e-mail?	그녀는 이메일을 받을 수 있니?
soon	곧	You have to go home soon.	너는 곧 집으로 가야만 한다.
hurry	서두르다	I have to hurry up.	나는 서둘러야만 한다.
cross	건너다	They can't cross the street.	그들은 그 거리를 건널 수 없다.
chopstick	젓가락	James can use the chopsticks.	James는 젓가락을 사용할 수 있다.
repeat	반복하다	She has to repeat the word.	그녀는 그 말을 반복해야만 한다.
history	역사	John will teach history.	John은 역사를 가르칠 것이다.
hunt	사냥하다	The king must hunt the big bear.	그 왕은 큰 곰을 사냥해야만 한다.
practice	연습하다	You don't have to practice soccer.	너는 축구를 연습할 필요가 없다.

meeting	회의	Tom was late for the meeting.	Tom은 그 회의에 늦었다.
fresh	신선한	The apples were fresh.	사과들은 신선했다.
close	친한	They were my close friends.	그들은 나의 친한 친구들이었다.
wallet	지갑	She bought a wallet yesterday.	그녀는 어제 지갑을 샀다.
fight	싸우다	They fought each other yesterday.	그들은 어제 서로 싸웠다.
sunflower	해바라기	I drew sunflowers last night.	나는 어젯밤에 해바라기를 그렸다.
build	짓다	Tony built the house last month.	Tony는 지난 달에 그 집을 지었다.
treasure	보물	He found the treasure last fall.	그는 지난 가을에 보물을 발견했다.
begin	시작하다	The school begins at nine o'clock.	그 학교는 9시에 시작한다.
broken	부서진	My father fixes the broken bike.	나의 아버지는 부서진 자전거를 고친다.
cold	감기	Julie caught a bad cold.	Julie는 심한 감기에 걸렸다.
gate	대문	They stand in front of the gate.	그들은 그 대문 앞에서 서 있다.
voice	목소리	Tony and Brian heard her voice.	Tony와 Brian은 그녀의 목소리를 들었다.
postcard	엽서	She wrote a postcard to her father.	그녀는 그녀의 아버지에게 엽서를 썼다.
free	자유로운	They were free last Saturday.	그들은 지난 토요일에 비번이었다.
way	길	I knew the way to the hospital.	나는 병원으로 가는 길을 알았다.
lose	잃어버리다	He lost his watch last year.	그는 작년에 그의 시계를 잃어버렸다.
city hall	시청	He drove to the city hall yesterday.	그는 어제 시청으로 차를 몰고 갔다.
invent	발명하다	King Sejong invented Hangeul in 1443.	세종대왕은 1443년에 한글을 발명했다.
bottom	바닥	Water flows from the top to the bottom.	물은 위에서 바닥으로 흐른다.
airport	공항	She arrived at the airport four hours ago.	그녀는 4시간 전에 공항에 도착했다.
steal	훔치다	A thief stole money in my bag then.	그 때 한 도둑이 나의 가방에서 돈을 훔쳤다.
walk	산책	They took a walk three hours ago.	그들은 3시간 전에 산책을 했다.
pay	지불하다	Kate paid twenty dollars for it then.	Kate는 그때 그것을 위해 20달러를 지불했다
poem	시	He read the poem before.	그는 전에 그 시를 읽었다.
coin	동전	Bill collected the many coins then.	Bill은 그때 많은 동전을 모았다.
rope	밧줄	Mark cut the rope with a knife.	Mark는 칼로 밧줄을 잘랐다.
end	끝나다	The class ended at three p.m. yesterday.	그 수업은 어제 오후 3시에 끝났다.
hurt	다치다	Emily hurt her arm last Saturday.	Emily는 지난 토요일에 그녀의 팔을 다쳤다.
magazine	잡지	He read the magazine in the afternoon.	그는 오후에 그 잡지를 읽었다.

luggage	짐	They carried the luggage into the room.	그들은 그 방으로 그 짐을 운반했다.
spend	소비하다	She spent a lot of money then.	그녀는 그때 많은 돈을 소비했다.
crosswalk	횡단보도	I stopped in front of the crosswalk.	나는 횡단보도 앞에서 멈췄다.
crop	농작물	The farmer sold the crops to the market.	그 농부는 시장에 그 농작물들을 팔았다.
dictionary	사전	Judy gave him a new dictionary.	Judy는 그에게 새로운 사전을 줬다.
cabin	오두막	He built the cabin with them.	그는 그들과 함께 오두막을 지었다.
lying	거짓말	People believed the boy's lying.	사람들은 그 소년의 거짓말을 믿었다.
interested	관심 있는	He was interested in soccer.	그는 축구에 관심이 있었다.
afraid	두려워하는	Susan was afraid of dogs.	Susan은 개를 두려워했다.
sneaker	운동화	Your sneakers were very dirty.	너의 운동화는 매우 더러웠다.
bowl	사발, 그릇	The tomatoes were in the bowl.	그 토마토들은 그 사발에 있었다.
fishing	낚시	My family went fishing last week.	나의 가족은 지난주에 낚시를 갔다.
call	전화하다	His brother called you last week.	그의 형이 지난주에 너에게 전화를 했다.
education	교육	Matt was interested in the education.	Matt은 교육에 관심이 있었다.
blouse	블라우스	Mrs. Smith wore a white blouse.	Smith 여사는 흰 블라우스를 입었다.
save	저축하다	They saved money for her birthday.	그들은 그녀의 생일을 위해 돈을 모았다.
hole	구멍	Bill and Tom found the big hole.	Bill과 Tom은 큰 구멍을 발견했다.
sound	소리	Did she hear the strange sound?	그녀는 이상한 소리를 들었니?
break	깨뜨리다	He broke the window yesterday.	그는 어제 창문을 깨뜨렸다.
kick	차다	Thomas kicked the ball in the park.	Thomas는 공원에서 공을 찼다.
diary	일기	My sister wrote the diary last night.	나의 여동생은 지난밤에 일기를 썼다.
visitor	방문객	The visitor saw towers there.	그 방문객은 거기서 탑들을 보았다.
mistake	실수	Kate made the same mistake.	Kate는 똑같은 실수를 했다.
driver	운전사	The drivers were busy and tired.	그 운전기사들은 바쁘고 지쳤다.
lunch box	도시락	I went there with a lunch box.	나는 도시락을 가지고 거기에 갔다.
riddle	수수께끼	Mark solved the riddle.	Mark는 그 수수께끼를 풀었다.
cave	동굴	The bats lived in this cave.	그 박쥐들은 이 동굴에서 살았다.
shelf	선반	Tom put the book on the shelf.	Tom은 선반 위에 그 책을 놓았다.
field	들판	The farmers were on the field.	그 농부들은 들판에 있었다.
judge	재판관	The judge punished the bad man.	그 재판관은 그 나쁜 남자를 벌주었다.

bug	벌레	He was catching some bugs.	그는 조금의 벌레들을 잡고 있었다.
jean	청바지	She and he were wearing jeans.	그녀와 그는 청바지를 입고 있었다.
resemble	닮다	Thomas resembles his father.	Thomas는 그의 아버지를 닮았다.
belong	소유이다	This book belonged to me.	이 책은 나의 소유였다.
rock	바위	You were sitting on a rock.	너는 바위 위에 앉았다.
china	도자기	I touch the china.	나는 그 도자기를 만진다.
truck	트럭	Jonathan was driving a truck.	Jonathan은 트럭을 운전하고 있었다.
draw	그리다	Dan was drawing a picture.	Dan은 그림을 그리고 있었다.
kite	연	Eric was flying a kite on the hill.	Eric은 언덕에서 연을 날리고 있었다.
guidebook	안내서	Amy read the guidebook.	Amy는 안내서를 읽었다.
silver	은	The people brought much silver.	그 사람들은 많은 은을 가져왔다.
dragonfly	잠자리	We caught the dragonfly.	우리는 잠자리를 잡았다.
together	함께	They were having lunch together.	그들은 함께 점심을 먹고 있었다.
gym	체육관	Nick exercised at the gym.	Nick은 체육관에서 운동했다.
hotel	호텔	The men stayed at the hotel.	그 남자들은 호텔에 머물렀다.
lemonade	레모네이드	Judy drank lemonade.	Judy는 레모네이드를 마셨다.
dig	파다	You dug a big hole.	너는 큰 구멍을 팠다.
language	언어	Cathy studied two languages.	Cathy는 2개의 언어를 배웠다.
bark	짖다	The dog was barking at him.	그 개는 그를 향해 짖고 있었다.
shower	샤워	Tom was taking a shower.	Tom은 샤워를 하고 있었다.
donut	도넛	Dan and Ann were selling donuts.	Dan과 Ann은 도넛을 팔고 있었다.
snowman	눈사람	We were making snowmen.	우리는 눈사람들을 만들고 있었다.
kitchen	부엌	He cooks in the kitchen.	그는 부엌에서 요리한다.
text	본문, 문서	Joseph sends a text message.	Joseph은 문자 메시지를 보낸다.
fork	포크	My son puts forks on the table.	나의 아들은 탁자 위에 포크를 놓는다.
player	운동선수	The player hit the ball.	그 운동선수는 공을 찼다.
office	사무실	He was coming to my office.	그는 나의 사무실로 오고 있었다.
hug	껴안다	The kid was hugging the teddy bear.	그 어린이는 그 곰 인형을 껴 안고 있었다.
pet	애완동물	They had a lot of pets.	그들은 많은 애완동물을 가지고 있었다.
yard	마당	We had a beautiful yard.	우리는 아름다운 마당을 가지고 있었다.

invite	초대하다	John will invite his friends.	John은 그의 친구들을 초대할 것이다.
hometown	고향	I will go back to my hometown.	나는 나의 고향으로 돌아갈 것이다.
arrive	도착하다	She will arrive here tomorrow.	그녀는 내일 여기에 도착할 것이다.
barbecue	바비큐	We will have a barbecue party.	우리는 바비큐 파티를 할 것이다.
land	착륙하다	The plane will land in Seoul in an hour.	그 비행기는 1시간 안에 착륙할 것이다.
high school	고등학교	My brother is a high school student.	나의 오빠는 고등학생이다.
warm	따뜻한	It will be warm next weekend.	다음 주말은 따뜻할 것이다.
attend	참석하다	She is going to attend the meeting.	그녀는 그 미팅에 참석할 것이다.
light	전등	We are going to turn off the lights.	우리는 그 전등들을 끌 것이다.
fire station	소방서	I walk to the fire station.	나는 소방서로 걸어간다.
join	가입하다	Alex will join the club.	Alex는 그 클럽에 가입할 것이다.
fine	맑은, 좋은	It will be fine tomorrow.	내일은 맑을 것이다.
paint	칠하다	She is going to paint the house soon.	그녀는 곧 집을 칠할 것이다.
surprised	놀란	They will be surprised at the news.	그들은 그 뉴스에 놀랄 것이다.
wine	포도주	Jess will bring some wine next week.	Jess는 다음 주에 와인을 가져올 것이다.
truth	진실	She will tell him about the truth.	그녀는 그에게 진실을 말할 것이다.
chance	기회	My father will give me a chance.	나의 아버지는 나에게 기회를 줄 것이다.
barber	이발사	The barber will cut his hair soon.	그 이발사는 곧 그의 머리카락을 자를 것이다.
department store	백화점	I meet her in the department store.	나는 그녀를 백화점에서 만난다.
trip	여행	I am going to take a trip.	나는 여행을 할 것이다.
bake	굽다	We bake some bread.	우리는 조금의 빵을 굽는다.
order	주문하다	He will order many books.	그는 많은 책을 주문할 것이다.
picnic	소풍	They go on a picnic to the river.	그들은 강으로 소풍을 간다.
clearly	명확히	We can see the star clearly.	우리는 그 별을 명확히 볼 수 있다.
musician	음악가	He is a famous musician.	그는 유명한 음악가이다.
job	직업	He is going to have a job.	그는 직업을 가질 것이다.
disappear	사라지다	She will disappear after the show.	그녀는 쇼 후에 사라질 것이다.
life	삶, 생명	He is going to enjoy his life.	그는 그의 삶을 즐길 것이다.
report	보고서	She will help me with my report.	그녀는 나의 보고서 작성을 도울 것이다.
dentist	치과의사	He will be a good dentist.	그는 훌륭한 치과의사가 될 것이다.

다음 우리말 뜻에 맞는 영어 단어를 쓰시오.

1 3월 _____

2 2월 _____

3 1월 _____

4 4월 _____

5 소수점, 점 _____

6 6월 _____

7 5월 _____

8 8월 _____

9 9월 _____

10 10월 _____

11 11월 _____

12 12월 _____

13 7월 _____

14 배, 몇 번 _____

15 2분의 1, 반 _____

다음 우리말 뜻에 맞는 영어 단어를 쓰시오.

1 버스 정류장 _____

2 모으다 _____

3 4분의 1 _____

4 선 _____

5 등급, 학년 _____

6 보내다 _____

7 손가락 _____

8 바구니 _____

9 엽서 _____

10 식사 _____

11 단추, 버튼 _____

12 분 _____

13 식목일 _____

14 층 _____

15 마루, 층 _____

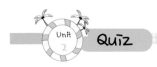
다음 우리말 뜻에 맞는 영어 단어를 쓰시오.

1 숨기다 _____

2 빌리다 _____

3 우표 _____

4 금발의 _____

5 ～을 준비하다 _____

6 기 _____

7 지갑 _____

8 ～을 운반하다 _____

9 단지 _____

10 빈 _____

11 야구 방망이 _____

12 강당 _____

13 ～ 의 사이에 _____

14 조용한 _____

15 질문하다 _____

다음 우리말 뜻에 맞는 영어 단어를 쓰시오.

1 이웃　　　　　_____

2 변호사　　　　_____

3 작동하다　　　_____

4 정보　　　　　_____

5 소설　　　　　_____

6 소개하다　　　_____

7 편지　　　　　_____

8 타다　　　　　_____

9 인기 배우　　　_____

10 여행하다　　　_____

11 떨어지다　　　_____

12 사교적인　　　_____

13 두꺼운　　　　_____

14 움직이다　　　_____

15 믿다　　　　　_____

다음 우리말 뜻에 맞는 영어 단어를 쓰시오.

1   마른 _____

2   어두운 _____

3   가는, 얇은 _____

4   아픈 _____

5   특별한 _____

6   바쁜 _____

7   현명한 _____

8   유명한 _____

9   싼 _____

10   뚱뚱한 _____

11   조심스러운 _____

12   이상한 _____

13   무거운 _____

14   사랑스러운 _____

15   더운 _____

다음 우리말 뜻에 맞는 영어 단어를 쓰시오.

1	단단한	_____
2	유용한	_____
3	위험한	_____
4	젖은	_____
5	과목	_____
6	일찍	_____
7	일어나다	_____
8	북극	_____
9	산	_____
10	섬	_____
11	용감한	_____
12	강철	_____
13	예의 바른	_____
14	장소	_____
15	두꺼운	_____

다음 우리말 뜻에 맞는 영어 단어를 쓰시오.

1 구조하다 _____

2 운동하다 _____

3 규칙 _____

4 이해하다 _____

5 홀로 _____

6 수리하다 _____

7 청소하다 _____

8 머무르다 _____

9 역 _____

10 오늘밤 _____

11 스페인어 _____

12 기타 _____

13 운반하다 _____

14 시험 _____

15 조부모 _____

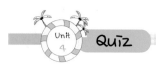

다음 우리말 뜻에 맞는 영어 단어를 쓰시오.

1	쓰레기	_____
2	~를 이기다	_____
3	주말	_____
4	씹다	_____
5	선물	_____
6	강당	_____
7	건강	_____
8	모형	_____
9	표	_____
10	(차를) 운전하다	_____
11	교과서	_____
12	이탈리아의	_____
13	성	_____
14	복종하다	_____
15	신문	_____

다음 우리말 뜻에 맞는 영어 단어를 쓰시오.

1	짓다	_____
2	콘서트	_____
3	회의	_____
4	선물	_____
5	부서진	_____
6	지갑	_____
7	친한	_____
8	해바라기	_____
9	대문	_____
10	보물	_____
11	싸우다	_____
12	(~을) 시작하다	_____
13	지하철	_____
14	감기	_____
15	신선한	_____

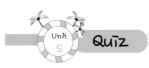

다음 우리말 뜻에 맞는 영어 단어를 쓰시오.

1   자유로운   _____

2   엽서   _____

3   지불하다   _____

4   길   _____

5   시청   _____

6   떠나다   _____

7   발명하다   _____

8   움직이다   _____

9   목소리   _____

10   바닥   _____

11   서점   _____

12   훔치다   _____

13   공항   _____

14   산책   _____

15   (~을) 잃어버리다   _____

다음 우리말 뜻에 맞는 영어 단어를 쓰시오.

	짐	
2	소비하다	
3	관심이 있는	
4	농작물	
5	사전	
6	개구리	
7	소방관	
8	거짓말	
9	횡단보도	
10	비싼	
11	오두막	
12	목이 마른	
13	운동화	
14	두려워하는	
15	도움	

다음 우리말 뜻에 맞는 영어 단어를 쓰시오.

1　캐나다　_____

2　비싼　_____

3　그릇, 사발　_____

4　저축하다　_____

5　블라우스　_____

6　구멍　_____

7　미술관　_____

8　벌주다　_____

9　소리　_____

10　야채　_____

11　깨뜨리다　_____

12　전화하다　_____

13　낚시　_____

14　극장　_____

15　교육　_____

다음 우리말 뜻에 맞는 영어 단어를 쓰시오.

1	마당	_____
2	청바지	_____
3	안내서	_____
4	소유이다	_____
5	바위	_____
6	눈사람	_____
7	그리다	_____
8	트럭	_____
9	벌레	_____
10	연	_____
11	언덕	_____
12	은	_____
13	체육관	_____
14	운동선수	_____
15	잠자리	_____

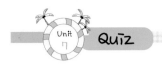

다음 우리말 뜻에 맞는 영어 단어를 쓰시오.

1 부엌 _____

2 레모네이드 _____

3 호텔 _____

4 언어 _____

5 문서, 본문 _____

6 샤워 _____

7 짖다 _____

8 도자기 _____

9 도넛 _____

10 웃다 _____

11 파다 _____

12 포크 _____

13 껴안다 _____

14 사무실 _____

15 함께 _____

다음 우리말 뜻에 맞는 영어 단어를 쓰시오.

1 치과의사 _____

2 초대하다 _____

3 휴식 _____

4 도착하다 _____

5 주문하다 _____

6 착륙하다 _____

7 바비큐 _____

8 따뜻한 _____

9 좋은, 맑은 _____

10 목수 _____

11 전등 _____

12 소방서 _____

13 시골 _____

14 이발사 _____

15 참석하다 _____

다음 우리말 뜻에 맞는 영어 단어를 쓰시오.

1 포도주 _____

2 놀란 _____

3 백화점 _____

4 끝나다 _____

5 소풍 _____

6 기회 _____

7 진실 _____

8 가입하다 _____

9 따르다 _____

10 모래 _____

11 (~을) 굽다 _____

12 코트 _____

13 여행 _____

14 고등학교 _____

15 칠하다 _____

Answer Key

Unit 1 | Quiz 1회   p. 10

1 March 2 February 3 January 4 April
5 point 6 June 7 May 8 August
9 September 10 October 11 November
12 December 13 July 14 time 15 half

Unit 1 | Quiz 2회   p. 11

1 bus stop 2 collect 3 quarter 4 line
5 grade 6 send 7 finger 8 basket
9 postcard 10 meal 11 button
12 minute 13 Arbor Day 14 story
15 floor

Unit 2 | Quiz 1회   p. 12

1 hide 2 borrow 3 stamp 4 blond
5 prepare 6 flag 7 purse 8 carry
9 only 10 empty 11 bat 12 hall
13 among 14 silent 15 ask

Unit 2 | Quiz 2회   p. 13

1 neighbor 2 lawyer 3 work
4 information 5 novel 6 introduce
7 letter 8 ride 9 star 10 travel 11 drop
12 outgoing 13 thick 14 move
15 believe

Unit 3 | Quiz 1회   p. 14

1 dry 2 dark 3 thin 4 ill 5 special
6 busy 7 wise 8 popular 9 cheap
10 fat 11 careful 12 strange 13 heavy
14 lovely 15 hot

Unit 3 | Quiz 2회   p. 15

1 hard 2 useful 3 dangerous 4 wet
5 subject 6 early 7 get up
8 the North pole 9 mountain 10 island
11 brave 12 steel 13 polite 14 place
15 thick

Unit 4 | Quiz 1회   p. 16

1 rescue 2 exercise 3 rule
4 understand 5 alone 6 fix 7 clean
8 stay 9 station 10 tonight 11 Spanish
12 guitar 13 carry 14 exam
15 grandparent

Unit 4 | Quiz 2회   p. 17

1 garbage 2 win 3 weekend 4 chew
5 present 6 hall 7 health 8 model
9 ticket 10 drive 11 textbook 12 Italian
13 castle 14 obey 15 newspaper

Unit 5 ı Quiz 1회   p. 18

1 build   2 concert   3 meeting   4 gift
5 broken   6 wallet   7 close   8 sunflower
9 gate   10 treasure   11 fight   12 begin
13 subway   14 cold   15 fresh

Unit 5 ı Quiz 2회   p. 19

1 free   2 postcard   3 pay   4 way
5 city hall   6 leave   7 invent   8 move
9 voice   10 bottom   11 bookstore
12 steal   13 airport   14 walk   15 lose

Unit 6 ı Quiz 1회   p. 20

1 luggage   2 spend   3 interested   4 crop
5 dictionary   6 frog   7 fire fighter   8 lying
9 crosswalk   10 expensive   11 cabin
12 thirsty   13 sneaker   14 afraid   15 help

Unit 6 ı Quiz 2회   p. 21

1 Canada   2 expensive   3 bowl   4 save
5 blouse   6 hole   7 gallery   8 punish
9 sound   10 vegetable   11 break 12 call
13 fishing   14 theater   15 education

Unit 7 ı Quiz 1회   p. 22

1 yard   2 jeans   3 guidebook   4 belong
5 rock   6 snowman   7 draw   8 truck
9 bug   10 kite   11 hill   12 silver   13 gym
14 player   15 dragonfly

Unit 7 ı Quiz 2회   p. 23

1 kitchen   2 lemonade   3 hotel
4 language   5 text   6 shower   7 bark
8 china   9 donut   10 laugh   11 dig
12 fork   13 hug   14 office   15 together

Unit 8 ı Quiz 1회   p. 24

1 dentist   2 invite   3 rest   4 arrive
5 order   6 land   7 barbecue   8 warm
9 fine   10 carpenter   11 light
12 fire station   13 country   14 barber
15 attend

Unit 8 ı Quiz 2회   p. 25

1 wine   2 surprised   3 department store
4 end   5 picnic   6 chance   7 truth
8 join   9 follow   10 sand   11 bake
12 coat   13 trip   14 high school   15 paint

Memo

초등 영어 교재의 베스트셀러

초등 영어 문법 실력 쌓기!

Grammar Builder 3

Words in Grammar

Grammar
Builder
시리즈

UK

You Are the Only One!

Iam books